Adoption, Identity, and Kinship

ADOPTION, IDENTITY, AND KINSHIP

The Debate over Sealed Birth Records

KATARINA WEGAR

Yale University Press   New Haven and London

Portions of Chapter 3 appeared in "Adoption and Mental Health: A
Theoretical Critique of the Psychopathological Model," *American Journal
of Orthopsychiatry 65,* no. 4 (October 1995): 540–48.

Published with assistance from the Louis Stern Fund.

Library of Congress Cataloging-in-Publication Data
Wegar, Katarina.
Adoption, identity, and kinship : the debate over sealed birth records /
Katarina Wegar.
p.   cm.
Includes bibliographical references and index.
ISBN 0-300-06759-3 (alk. paper)
1. Adoption—United States.   2. Birthparents—United States—
Identification.   3. Adoptees—United States—Identification.
4. Confidential communications—United States.   5. Registers of births,
etc.—United States.   I. Title.
HV875.55.W44   1996
362.7'34—dc20   96-8145
                                                    CIP

Printed in the United States of America.

A catalogue record for this book is
available from the British Library.

The paper in this book meets the guidelines
for permanence and durability of the Committee
on Production Guidelines for Book Longevity of
the Council on Library Resources.

10 9 8 7 6 5 4 3 2 1

Contents

PREFACE

Sociological studies typically begin with methodological overviews intended to convince the readers that the analysis is based on rules and scripts that are shared and accepted by the scholarly community and that the conclusions offered do not simply reflect the researcher's personal experience or biased opinion. Unfortunately, this laudable attempt to separate inquiry from opinion has led many researchers to deny the connections between our scholarly interests and the passions and struggles of our lives. For some time in the history of sociology, emotional detachment from the subject under study has served as a primary marker of scientific objectivity. Yet, as critics of this unattainable ideal have noted, the line between mere intellectual curiosity and personal and political involvement always remains superficial in some respects.

Although I do not pretend to disclose in this preface the full extent of the influence of my life on my work, I want to take the opportunity to explain how I came to study the ongoing sealed records debate. As an adoptee and a student of sociology, I became interested in using the intellectual tools of sociology to understand adoption as an experience and an institution. This seemed like an especially worthwhile undertaking since, as I was quite astonished to discover, the subject of adoption has been largely neglected by sociologists. From my perspective as a Finnish graduate student in the United States, I found the debate over American adoptees' rights to gain identifying information about their biological parents particularly intriguing.

I was surprised to find that only three states, Alaska, Kansas, and Tennessee (Hollinger 1993, 52), currently grant adoptees the unequivocal right to acquire this information.

In contrast, Finland was one of the first countries in the Western world to allow adoptees access to identifying information. This policy, which had been implemented long before my birth, allowed me to identify my birth parents, and I remain in steady contact with my birth mother. The need for confidentiality, which American policymakers had for so long taken for granted, seemed rather peculiar to me, and my first attempts to grapple with adoption from a sociological perspective were aimed at understanding the logic behind the sealed records practice. Based on my own experience as an adoptee who had always taken access to identifying information for granted, the arguments against adoption reform did not make much sense. Although I recognized some problems with retroactive changes in adoption laws and procedures, this legal dilemma was not enough to convince me of the necessity of continued confidentiality. I could not readily accept the claim made by one of the leading advocates for closed records that the practice of sealing the adoptee's original birth records had made "the American pattern of adoption . . . far and away the most successful in the world" (Foster 1979, 35).

As I continued to explore the sealed records debate, however, I became increasingly interested in detangling the arguments in favor of the status quo as well as those in favor of open records. Both camps in the debate embrace arguments worth analyzing. The line of reasoning that has guided the institutionalization of adoption in the United States has largely ignored the experiences of adoptees, birth mothers and, to a certain extent, birth fathers. As a result, the legal right of adoptees to know their birth parents has been denied, and their desire to do so has been dismissed. In addition, birth mothers have been expected to disclaim the experience of birth and childbearing. The other line of reasoning, espoused by the advocates of the open adoption movement, assumes that there are certain universal character traits and instinctual behavior patterns that are shared by all adoptees, to varying degrees. The source of these traits and behavior patterns has typically been located within the adoptive family or the fact of the adoption itself.

The issue of "difference" enters the debate over openness in adoption in various ways. Researchers who have studied mental health issues in adoption have typically assumed that adoptees are different, and they have attributed this difference to the absence of biological bonds in the adoptive family (see chap. 3). Those adoption experts and policymakers who favor continued secrecy or confidentiality in adoption have treated adoptees differently from persons who are not adopted by denying them the right to know their biological roots, even though adoptees had no say in the original adoption decision. Curiously, the sealed records policy implies that the need to know may indeed exist but that it should be stifled. Proponents of the rights approach to adoption reform, on the other hand, have tended to reinforce the dominant cultural view of adoptees as different and deviant, as less than whole human beings. In a way, of course, we are different. But because pathology in our society is a central marker for difference, those who are considered different in some way are usually also labeled deviant and pathological. This is certainly true in the case of adoption (see chap. 5).

In contrast to most previous analyses and comments on adoption and the sealed records controversy, I argue that to claim that adoptees are different calls for a critical exploration of the social construction of difference and the family and kinship ideals from which adoptees and their families are thought to diverge. Although I take very seriously the desire of adoptees to know their biological origins, I challenge the ideological assumptions and the practical and political consequences of what I call the "new psychology of the adopted." Most commentators, researchers, and activists have tended to cut off experiences of adoption from the cultural contexts in which these experiences are embedded. Personal accounts are certainly valid sources of knowledge, but they cannot be understood apart from the cultural vocabularies in which they are formulated. In my view, any account of experiences of adoption that ignores the cultural symbolism and stigmatization of adoption runs the danger of unintentionally reproducing the structures and stereotypes it sets out to debunk. It is useful in this context to recall Roland Barthes's dictum: "Setting the stereotype at a distance is not a political task, for political language is itself made up of stereotypes, but a critical task, one, that is, which aims to call all language into crisis" (1977, 199).

It is not surprising that the practice of adoption is currently the focus of heated public debate. After all, the institution of adoption can reflect and represent the most tragic of injustices—the predicament of mothers compelled to give up their children for reasons beyond their choosing. At the same time, adoptive relationships can affirm the marvelous human capacity to feel and create kinship. These two aspects of adoption are so obvious and important that they cannot be disregarded or dismissed, as many of those involved in the current policy debate unfortunately have done. Perhaps there is something about the nature of public debates in our society that invites debaters to reason in terms of intransigence. As Albert O. Hirschman (1991) has noted regarding the nature of "democratic" disputes, progressives and reactionaries tend to employ surprisingly similar rhetorical postures. Perhaps it is the naive belief that an emancipatory goal can justify any means, as if the means and the end were fully separable in the first place. This book came about as the result of my concern that the goal to allow adoptees to choose the amount of information they want about their biological kin might be subverted by the means used to achieve this goal.

In this book, I approach the search debate from a frame-critical[1] perspective; that is, I explore the implicit "structures of belief, perception and appreciation" that shape the controversy (Schön and Rein 1994, 23). My analysis entails several theoretical assumptions. I assume (1) that public debates involve frames and dimensions that are seldom recognized but are nevertheless crucial because they help claims makers formulate convincing arguments by appealing to broad cultural themes and widely accepted understandings; (2) that personal histories or self-narratives, like any form of self-understanding, are social constructions reflecting a culture's narrative reserve and commonly held beliefs; and (3) that culture is the result of an active process rather than a fixed set of beliefs and that the search debate both reveals and is fueled by the ambiguity or indeterminacy of such central social concepts as kinship, family, and identity.

First I consider the social conditions that propelled the emergence of the search movement in the 1960s and 1970s. Chapter 2 briefly outlines the background of the current debate by reviewing the historical development of adoption as a social institution in the United States and elsewhere. It also reviews the legal challenges to the sealed records policy and examines how these challenges have been met. Furthermore, it summarizes existing critiques of the American adoption system and

1. For a brief overview of the frame-analytical approach, see Gamson et al. (1992).

the ways in which this system and the sealed records policy have perpetuated inequalities of gender, race, and class.

Chapter 3 provides an overview of research on adoption, from the early studies of adoption pathology to the most recent studies on searching. The main trend in adoption research reflects the normative assumption that dilemmas of adoption result from individual shortcomings (which ultimately have a biological or instinctual basis) rather than from the structure of adoption as a social institution. For example, studies of adoption and mental health have so far focused mainly on psychodynamic processes, while the cultural and institutional factors that generate the psychological dilemmas have remained opaque. Adoption research has thus covertly characterized the adoptive family as an aberrant type, as an entity that is problematic or pathogenic in itself. Although search activists have questioned the conventional wisdom of adoption experts, they have continued to view dilemmas of adoption largely as the result of individual pathology, in line with the dominant paradigm of adoption research. Chapter 3 also considers how the "professional project" of child welfare workers (Larson 1977) has shaped adoption theory and practice.

Drawing on articles in social work journals, activist newsletters, and autobiographies by prominent members of the search movement, in chapter 4 I analyze the rhetorical role and nature of self-narratives in the search debate. A key to the relative success of the reformers' claims (at least when it comes to making adoption a public issue) has been their ability to convert the issue of confidentiality into one of secrecy. In this process of reframing, a practice that was formerly represented in positive terms has been invested with negative social meanings (see Gamson et al. 1992). This transformation has been made possible by phrasing claims in favor of searching in terms of moral themes in the culture at large. Three ideographs have pervaded the adoption reform activists' arguments: the significance of truth and personal authenticity, the significance of individual freedom and the right to (if not the moral obligation of) self-discovery, and the inviolability of the blood relation. The search activists and those who oppose adoption reform have drawn upon opposing interpretations of the same cultural symbols or ideographs. For example, both camps have argued that their views genuinely express the American ethos of individualism.

Chapter 5 continues to analyze the symbolic dimension of the search controversy by examining media coverage of the debate and popular accounts of adoption, as found in mystery novels and on talk shows. The basic structure of these texts represents adoptees and adoptive relations as similar yet different, and horror stories of searching epitomize this distinction. However, while representations of adoption on talk shows advance the biological definition of family and kinship, they also reveal tensions in the American family ideology. When audience members on *Donahue*, for example, argue that "love is not biological" (*Donahue* 1991, 21), they implicitly refute the view that blood ties are enough to make a family. The chapter also considers the relevance of the search debate for the ongoing debate over the fate and future of the American family.

The final chapter takes up the problems and potentials of a feminist critique of adoption. The chapter relates the search debate to the struggle over the meaning and nature of motherhood and considers the usefulness of a feminist analysis of the debate. For feminists, motherhood has provided a prime site for exploring and contesting the boundaries of nature and culture, biology and identity. Yet, feminist researchers have seldom recognized the problematic situation of adoptive mothers from a gender perspective. Rather, they have taken the position that the experiences of these women are determined by their class position. Chapter 6 also summarizes the issues surrounding the paradox of emancipatory rhetoric—that is, the possibility that rhetorical success might limit rather than promote social change. As Martha Minow (1990, 237) has remarked, an emancipatory agenda does not make reformers immune to "adopt[ing] categories that others have used and at times reinforc[ing] particular prejudices and general modes of argument that assign difference to others and ignore the social meaning of the act of assignment." In conclusion I consider the possibilities of arguing for adoption reform from a sociological and interactionist point of view by accounting for both the natural and the social elements of kinship and identity without perpetuating stereotypical images of those most intimately affected by adoption.

Several individuals have helped me in my endeavor to write this book. Among those I count most are the friends and acquaintances with whom I have discussed my work. In particular I wish to thank the three members of my dissertation committee at Brandeis University, Irving Kenneth Zola, Maurice Stein, and Shulamit Reinharz, for their continuous guidance and support as I wrote the doctoral thesis that constitutes the foundation of this book. I feel especially fortunate to have benefited from Irv Zola's guidance and wisdom before his death, in the winter of 1994. He was the first to encourage me to pursue the adoption topic, and he tirelessly guided me along the way. The support of all my advisers at Brandeis extended far beyond the specific problems of writing a dissertation and has often worked in subtle but invaluable ways. The mere presence of scholars who in their own work and teaching have successfully linked the scholarly, the personal, and the political has been of paramount importance, and I doubt that the impetus for this study would have come about without that influence. Christine Ward Gailey at Northeastern University has also offered expertise, inspiration, and help beyond the standard requirements of academic relationships.

Several other members of the faculty and staff at the Brandeis University Sociology Department contributed with help and suggestions for this project. I would in particular like to thank Peter Conrad and Kurt H. Wolff for their interest and encouragement. By encouraging me to write and think sociologically in the first place, Elianne Riska of Abo Akademi University, Finland, offered support long before this project was under way, and she has continued to offer helpful comments on my work.

I am also grateful for the expertise of Gladys Topkis of Yale University Press and of Karen Gangel, the manuscript editor. Their enthusiasm and meticulous reading of the manuscript have been invaluable in bringing this book to fruition.

Finally, I owe a particular debt to my friends Mark Simonoff and Patricia Sardella, who supported me during the writing process. Mark read and commented on parts of the manuscript as well. Last but decidedly not least, I thank my parents, Karin and Martin Wegar, who in addition to their untiring and loving support have shared with me their wise understanding of the complexities of adoption.

Adoption, Identity, and Kinship

I

Introduction

ADOPTION AND THE

DIFFERENCE DILEMMA

Activists who strive for social change face a fundamental strategic and moral dilemma. On the one hand, arguments that resonate with existing values and beliefs generally are more convincing and therefore more effective than those that challenge accepted wisdom. On the other hand, by using the traditional arguments, social activists risk reinforcing old stereotypes and labels of inferiority and difference.[1] This dilemma has shaped the ongoing debate over the right of adoptees to have access to identifying information about their biological parents—the so-called search or sealed records controversy. The failure to examine critically society's view of adoptees as similar to yet different from children who live with their biological parents has led the search movement to perpetuate confining images of adoption, kinship, and identity. In this respect the arguments of search activists follow the tradition of adoption research that has dominated public discourse on the topic. Neither side understands the experiences of adoption within a social context, and as a consequence both tend to pathologize adoptive kinship.

The search controversy has become part of a small, exclusive group of social issues that have gained increasing visibility in

1. Minow (1990) makes this point in her analysis of the difference dilemma in American law. I draw in particular on her analysis of the feminist-rights approach to legal equality.

the media. For the first time in the history of American adoption, the conflicting positions are being tested and played out against each other—in the popular media, in the social work and scientific community, and among legal scholars. Especially during the past decade, adoptees' quest for their origins has "generated a whole industry of fiction . . . plays, and semi-autobiographical films" (Triseliotis 1984, 41).

From one perspective, the search debate can be read as a conflict between two opposing stories. One story depicts the American adoption system as a benevolent force acting in the best interests of parentless children, as well as of their biological parents (code for birth mothers) and the adoptive parents. The other portrays the system as an oppressive institution that ignores and contradicts adoptees' real needs and interests. The first story dominated public discourse on adoption during the first half of this century, and the second rose to prominence in the early 1970s as a result of the protests of such activist groups as the Adoptees' Liberty Movement Association (ALMA), organized in 1971 by Florence Fisher.

From another perspective, however, the search activists and those who oppose open records appear to employ similar rhetorical postures. Although both factions have emphasized the issue of difference in adoption, they have failed to understand adoption in the context of difference. By dismissing adoptees' desire to search and by denying them the legal right to know their biological origins, advocates of closed records have treated them as different from persons who have not been adopted. Betty Jean Lifton (1994, 8), a prominent search activist, has written that "it is unnatural for members of the human species to grow up separated from and without knowledge of their natural clan." Unnatural or not, in matters of kinship and identity American society tends to attribute paramount importance to blood ties; in addition, the very existence of the sealed records policy implies that blood relations may be strong enough to threaten adoptive family bonds (Bartholet 1993, 58–59). In their challenge to this policy, search activists have claimed that adoption is inherently problematic and that adoptees are therefore fundamentally different from other children. Such a claim, however, calls for a critical exploration of the social construction of difference, the psychological impact of labels of difference (social stigmatization), and the ideals from which adoption and adoptees are thought to diverge.

The main objective of this book is to examine adoption and adoptees as socially and culturally constructed categories and to consider the place of these categories in the sealed records debate. This controversy has essentially concerned adult adoptees' right to obtain genealogical information without a court order or the consent of the birth parents, a right that currently is granted in only three states—Alaska, Kansas, and Tennessee (Hollinger 1993). A distinction has been made between the right to receive medical information concerning one's birth parents and the right to receive information that identifies one or both of them (DeWoody 1993). This book is concerned with the latter.

The search controversy should also be distinguished from the related debate over "open adoption," which "occurs when, prior to the adoption, it is agreed in writing that the child will have continuing contact with one or more members of his or her biological family after the adoption is completed" (Amadio and Deutsch 1983–84, 60). Although these issues are closely related, I focus primarily on searching, a topic that sociologists have largely neglected (as they have the study of adoption in general).

The first American adoption law was passed in Massachusetts in 1851; by 1925 all forty-eight states had enacted some type of adoption legislation. The Massachusetts law did not create the institution of adoption; it simply transformed the adoption proceeding from a private act to a general comprehensive statute that was publicly recognized and sanctioned. Emphasizing the child's best interest, the law required proof of the adopters' ability to parent as well as the written consent of the child's biological parents or legal guardian or of the adoptee if he or she was older than fourteen (Presser 1971, 465).

Beginning in Minnesota in 1917, the states progressively passed laws prohibiting the release of identifying information (see chap. 2). Protests against the sealed records policy were voiced at least as early as the 1950s, but the search movement did not receive widespread recognition until the 1970s. The movement currently consists of hundreds of local and national adoption support groups, most of which are members of the American Adoption Congress (AAC), the national umbrella organization founded in 1985. Also pressing for open records are birth parents (mostly mothers), who have formed Concerned United Birthparents (CUB). Statistics on adoption are sparse and unreliable, but it has been estimated that there are currently at least five million adopted individuals in the United States (Schulman and Behrman 1993, 6). No figures are available, however, on the number of adoptees or birth parents who search or wish to search for their unknown biological relatives.

Although adoption practice over the past twenty years has changed in the direction of greater openness, there is still great variety in the policies of agencies and the degrees of openness. In most states, legislation continues to support the principle of sealed records (Amadio 1991, 29). Although adoption agencies, child welfare organizations, and lobbyist groups such as the Child Welfare League of America and the National Committee for Adoption have traditionally opposed open records, some child welfare professionals have actively participated in the search movement.[2] On the other hand, not all adoptees want to search for their biological relatives, and some birth parents oppose the disclosure of identifying information. Search advocates have generally argued for adoptees' right to have access to their birth records upon demand, whereas such groups as the National Committee for Adoption have viewed the establishment of mutual-consent registries as sufficient or as the only fair solution. Significantly, the model Uniform Adoption Act, drafted by the National Conference of Commissioners on Uniform State Laws in 1994 and approved by the American Bar Association in 1995, does not recommend that records be opened upon demand.

Why Not a Sociology of Adoption?

The scholarly literature on adoption has been dominated by psychiatrists, psychologists, and child welfare workers who have explained problems that arise in adoptive families (especially mental health issues involving adoptees) in predominately individualistic terms, without taking into account the social factors and processes that affect adoption experiences and policies. With the notable exception of H. David Kirk, those sociologists who have studied adoption have chosen to focus on family interaction rather than to take the social institution of adoption as their starting point. Few textbooks on the sociology of the family have addressed adoption; those that have done so treat it mainly as a historical or anthropological curiosity or as a welfare service (Kirk 1985, 3). When adoption practices have

2. The National Committee for Adoption lobbies for the regulation and support of adoptions. This organization claims to protect the rights of all members of the adoption triangle but opposes open records. The Washington-based group was renamed the National Council for Adoption.

been subjected to comparative sociological research (Chambers 1975), historical description has tended to overshadow sociological interpretation.

In the 1970s, a number of researchers, noting that "problems in both foster care and adoption systems flow out of the problems of the larger society" (Mandell 1973, 3), began to address class and racial inequalities in the American adoption system. Despite this enlightened point of view, their analyses failed to encompass the cultural ideals of kinship and the family. Feminist critics of the adoption system have been more successful in exposing the social construction and normative ideals of the family and parenthood by revealing the impact of gender domination on adoption laws, which punish unwed birth mothers in particular (see chaps. 2 and 6). These adoption studies have, however, remained peripheral to the endeavors of sociologists studying the family.

The paucity of sociological studies of adoption, which at first glance appears quite surprising, deserves some critical reflection; neglected topics tend to reveal as much about a discipline as do its favorite subjects. First, sociologists' lack of interest in adoption reflects a tendency to take biocentric definitions of the family, kinship, and parenting for granted. According to the traditional American ideal, the family is defined as a natural or biological arrangement (Andersen 1991, 235), and despite the great variety of family forms (e.g., adoptive, foster, single-parent, stepparent), mainstream family sociologists have tended to disregard nontraditional and especially nonbiological family forms. Ironically, considering the long-standing feminist suspicion of essentialist definitions of womanhood, this biocentric bias has been reinforced by feminist researchers in recent years. As Elayne Rapping (1990, 541) has remarked regarding some feminist responses to the controversy over surrogacy, "a number of feminists—liberal, radical, and socialist—were suddenly arguing as vehemently for the rights of the biological mother and the sanctity of the biological bond between mother and child as they had once argued for the right not to mother." Similarly, Phyllis Chesler's *The Sacred Bond* (1989) and other recent feminist writings expose existing gender inequalities in the sphere of reproduction, but at times they also reinforce the same unquestioning acceptance of the "order of nature" that has characterized most mainstream sociological research on the family.

A second reason for the lack of sociological interest in adoption can be traced to traditional conceptions of what constitutes a social problem. In contrast to the related subject of illegitimacy (which emerged as a topic of sociological concern as early as the 1930s; Davis 1939–40), adoption has been traditionally defined not as a social problem but, rather, as the solution to one. Rather than challenging the social construction of social problems by experts and policymakers, sociologists seem to have accepted the dominant view of adoption as a necessary and benevolent response to the social problem of out-of-wedlock births. Policymakers have argued that adoption benefits society by relieving it of the financial burden of caring for "parent-less" children. But, as feminist critics have pointed out, unwed mothers have often paid a disproportionately high emotional price for this benefit.

A third reason for the virtual neglect of adoption in family sociology is, as Kirk (1985, 5) has noted, that adoption has not been classified as a cultural item in the same league as "family" and "kinship" but has instead been associated with "welfare services." As such, the study of adoption has been defined by academic sociologists as a less prestigious area of research, one that should be left to social workers. As a result, sociologists have missed the chance to challenge the lack of contextual grounding in the scholarly literature, including the lack of any serious consideration of the social stigmatization of adoption and the subsequent tendency to pathologize adoptive kinship.

The Search Movement

In some respects the search movement is a prototype of what has been called the new social movements. In contrast to the old social movements, the new movements "are not sparked by *problems of distribution,* but concern the *grammar of forms of life*" (Habermas 1981, 33). In contrast to the old politics of production and distribution, they express changes in attitudes and values relating to the quality of life, individual self-realization, and human rights.[3] Yet, the values represented by these social movements are not novel, as illustrated in the case of the search movement, which reflects the ethos of individual freedom, choice, and self-fulfillment, principles that are "part and parcel of dominant modern culture" (Offe 1985, 848–49).

Another characteristic of the new social movements is that they often involve "new or formerly weak dimensions of identity"; that is, they attempt to "reclaim a self robbed of its identity" and aspire to "empower members to 'name themselves'" (Johnston, Laraña, and Gusfield 1994, 7, 10). Stories about experiences of adoption and searching (which I call search narratives; see also Modell 1992, 79) have been crucial in reflecting the ethos of the search movement and redefining what it means to be adopted. The recounting of life stories has enabled adoptees to construct a new collective and public identity. Such

3. It is, however, misleading to make a sharp distinction between the old and the new social movements in this respect. The women's movement, and even the search movement to some extent, also strives to attain distributive justice. Perhaps this distinction reveals more about the dominant definition of "production and distribution" than about differences between the two types of social movements.

accounts have an important formative function, both personally and politically, "Stories give directions to lives" (Rosenwald and Ochberg 1992, 6). As Nancy Walker (1991, 3) noted in her discussion of the use of life stories in the women's movement, women's autobiographies "demonstrate conscious choices about which truth to tell, and when to remain silent. In doing so, they make manifest the woman's position as author of her own life, claiming the freedom to determine her own 'truth.' "

In contrast to versions of feminism and phenomenological sociology, which grant the author's experiences a privileged epistemological status by treating life stories as direct reflections of inner experiences and events (Silverman 1989, 38), Walker's account emphasizes the constructionist character of life stories. The constructionist approach (applied also in this book) stresses that self-understanding is always culturally shaped and framed. The difference between narratives and other types of verbal expression lies precisely in the way narratives help people to construct or make sense of their experiences, for themselves as well as for others (Riessman 1990, 116–19). Even life stories that have significant emancipatory potential, however, are not exempt from social influence or alternative forms of authority. Life stories told with a political or persuasive purpose run an even higher risk of reinforcing social convention. To convince the wider audience and policymakers of the necessity for social change, they must draw upon already established cultural vocabularies or "acceptable emotions" (Hahn and Gonchar 1971, 48).

Although rhetoric is a necessary element of public debates, the rhetorical imperative may also restrict political emancipation.[4] Public discourse certainly can generate social change,

---

4. Defined as a "matrix of meaning," the concept of discourse captures the interrelation among ideology, rhetoric, and the social construction

yet public persuasion typically presents partisan interests and agendas as universal. A constructionist approach links narrative analysis to a critical theory of society (Rosenwald and Ochberg 1992, 5). The constructionist approach to narrative analysis should not, however, lead to a devaluation or delegitimation of personal experience. Autobiographical narratives provide a means of expressing silenced experiences, such as the experiences of adoptees and birth mothers (and to some extent fathers) who have been denied the right to know their biological kin.

Public Debates as Frame Conflicts

Public controversies can be conceptualized as involving various frames or ways of seeing and interpreting reality. Frames are not arbitrary; they are rooted in broad systems of cultural belief and are further shaped by the institutions that sponsor them (Schön and Rein 1994). This rhetorical approach to public debates and social movements[5] can be traced to Kenneth Burke's dramatur-

---

of meaning. When sociologists speak of discourses, they typically mean discourses of knowledge. Like ideologies, the cognitive frameworks that shape a discourse are usually implicit and entail a "naturalization" of social reality: "the subject 'forgets' the discursive formation which sets him in place" (Eagleton 1991, 195-97). Historically, the study of rhetoric has been characterized by two opposing themes. According to one view, rhetoric is deficient and fallacious—epistemologically, morally, and socially. The other view defines rhetoric not as the antithesis to truth and morality but as an art or a means whereby facts are discovered rather than distorted (Fish 1989, 472).

5. Gusfield, for example, advanced this approach in his seminal work *Symbolic Crusade: Status Politics and the American Temperance Movement* (1963), in which he departs from previous sociological practice by exploring the implicit rather than explicit dimensions of social movement

gical perspective (1957, 267) and his contention that "politics is above all drama" and that social movements are essentially symbolic or rhetorical acts. The rhetorical approach to social movement research has since been developed in several directions; some authors have focused primarily on the persuasive role of leaders (e.g., Simons 1970), others on the role of rhetoric in social movement mobilization (e.g., Smith and Windes 1976). For the purposes of this book, the most useful finding stemming from this tradition of research is that in order to be maximally effective, claims for social change must match or draw upon the audience's "cultural heritage, that is their folk wisdom, narrations and myths" (Benford and Hunt 1992, 49). Thus "the *ethos* of a social movement can be enhanced by playing upon acceptable emotions. [For example,] Martin Luther King . . . improved the ethos of the civil rights movement by enunciating a 'dream' that exemplified the traditional American Dream" (Hahn and Gonchar 1971, 48).

The rhetorical approach has been applied in recent sociological analyses of the debate in the United States over women's right to abortion. In *Abortion and the Politics of Motherhood* (1985), Kristin Luker argued that the abortion debate concerns such social issues as family life, sexual norms, and the gendered division of labor. According to Luker, it is the implication of these broad structures of meaning in the abortion theme that have made the issue a topic of such fervent public controversy. Yet, as Celeste Condit (1990) noted, a common denominator of many studies of public controversies is that they tend to be nondiscursive; that is, they do not take into account the dy-

---

rhetoric. More recent examples of the frame-critical perspective include the work of Snow et al. (1986); Benford and Hunt (1992); and Gamson and Modigliani (1989).

namics of the persuasion process or the social force of rhetoric per se. Following Condit's suggestion, the analysis in this book attempts to illuminate the force of rhetoric in the process of social change. The emphasis on the symbolic dimension of the debate, upon which the success or failure of the search movement ultimately hinges, allows me to ask why the search issue has attracted so much media attention in recent years considering its specific and comparatively limited agenda and the possibly greater appeal of other human interest stories.

An analysis of the content of television dramas dealing with adoption indicates that searching has been drastically overrepresented (see chap. 3); the number of adoptees who decide to search in real life is far lower than the frequency of such programs would imply (Gerbner 1988, 3). On the one hand, media attention to the sealed records controversy is not novel but continues a preoccupation of Western society with the meaning of kinship, identity, and blood lineage that goes at least as far back as the Moses and Oedipus myths. On the other hand, the search controversy reveals concerns that are specific to American society in the late twentieth century, such as the changes in family stability that have fueled the ongoing political debate over the fate and future of the American family.

To understand the open records controversy, it is necessary to understand the paradigms that have informed adoption research. Since the 1960s, the courts have increasingly called upon "experts" in deciding cases that involve mental health issues (Mason 1994, 175), a trend that has also shaped the search debate. As I have pointed out, although search activists have challenged the dominant policy assumptions concerning sealed records, their arguments in some respects resemble those of their opponents, most of whom represent the state-sponsored adoption establishment. While the adoption institutions have followed rather than led the transition toward greater openness

(Caplan 1990, 49), the agenda of the search movement has been based on expert opinion to such an extent that the distinction between lay and expert discourse has been blurred. Popular and scientific beliefs are of course never strictly separated. Just as "intellectuals take up the concepts of everyday life and embellish them in their theorizing," so scientific concepts often filter through to popular texts and become accepted as common sense (Billig et al. 1988, 26).[6]

The Natural and Social Elements of Kinship

The sealed records controversy involves a struggle over conflicting definitions of the family, parenting, and identity. Although the American family ideal assumes that real families are constituted by blood (Andersen 1991; see also Bernardes 1985), the public debate over sealed records nevertheless reveals a tension between the natural and the social aspects of family life, kinship, identity, and bonding. The agenda of the search movement draws upon society's view of adoptees as simultaneously familiar, to the extent that the public can identify with their quest for identity, and different, to the extent that they are perceived as standing outside the order of nature, as Others. Search activists have attempted to overcome this gap by characterizing those adoptees who search as truly similar to other people—in that they share the human desire to connect with "one's own kind"—and by labeling adoptees who do not evince the wish to search as truly different. Thus searchers and nonsearchers have typically been approached as separate and fundamentally dif-

6. The long-standing dispute among scientists concerning the relative importance of nature and nurture for human behavior is one example of the complex relationship between social ideology and scientific theorizing (e.g., Lewontin, Rose, and Kamin 1984). This dispute has gained renewed urgency in the adoption controversy.

ferent groups, with respect to either their psychological predisposition or their experience of being adopted. By phrasing their arguments in terms of universal human needs, the activists have glossed over important experiential differences among adoptees with regard to both family relations and their sense of self. In order to confirm their collective and public identity, search activists have thus continued the long tradition in adoption discourse of disregarding the social relations in which experiences of adoption are embedded.

Adoption researchers and search activists have seldom taken seriously adoptees' conflicted attitudes toward issues of searching (Wegar 1992). Considering the ambivalence in society surrounding the relative significance of the biological and social elements of kinship, it is only to be expected that adoptees would harbor such feelings. Yet their experiences have been perceived as matters of personal inclination, not as historically and culturally embedded events. In this book I am primarily interested in the social context that shapes experiences of adoption. The focus is on sociological rather than psychological ambivalence, on contradiction at the institutional rather than personal level.

Some sociologists have interpreted experiences of ambiguity as symptoms of structural contradiction (as in Robert Merton's classic notion of "sociological ambivalence" [1976, 3–31]).[7] By and large, however, the idea of cultural coherence has dominated both sociological and anthropological approaches to the study of culture and society (Smelser 1992, 5), and the perception of what it feels like to live in the modern world has been dominated by a view of modern society as more or less void

7. A version of this view was also put forward by Mills (1940, 912) in his early work on the social character of motives; he argued that "mixed motives" or "motivational conflicts" have their origin in discrepant vocabularies of motive ("situated actions and vocabularies of motive").

of tension and contradiction (Giddens 1990, 137–44). Ideological thinking has often been regarded as devoid of incongruity,[8] although sociologists who focus on culture more than on ideology seem more likely to acknowledge contradiction.[9] Such an alternative approach was suggested by Kai Erikson (1976, 82) in his study of the destruction of community in the Buffalo Creek flood. Erikson argued that "the identifying motifs of a culture are not just the core values to which people pay homage but also the lines of point and counterpoint along which they diverge." Michael Billig and his colleagues (1988, 38) expressed the methodological consequences of this standpoint when they argued that the " 'spirit of the age' may be more accurately represented by the debate between two adversaries rather than by either party individually." Similarly, the search debate cannot be understood simply in terms of the dominant view in American society that kinship is defined by blood (Schneider 1980), because the debate also reflects the belief that feelings of kinship may transcend the blood relation.

Although public dialogue encourages conflict between different interpretations of truth and reality, at times it conceals

8. Proponents of the "dominant ideology thesis" in particular have tended to "overemphasize the degree of coherence, integration and stability" in society (Abercrombie, Hill, and Turner 1980, 6).

9. The reluctance of sociologists to examine social life as dilemma-ridden on the ideological level parallels a tendency among psychologists to view thinking exclusively in terms of "a desire for inner attitudinal harmony or in terms of the processing of incoming information." Festinger's theory of "cognitive dissonance" is a well-known example of this paradigm. Billig and his colleagues (1988, 20) have observed that schema theorists tend to "view thinking as what we do unthinkingly." Social psychologists who have focused on the experience of ambivalence have mostly defined it as a "painful condition" (Weigert and Franks 1989, 215), a social and mental state to be overcome and resolved. Ambivalence has furthermore been defined as a specifically modern experience, as "the temper of feeling our times" (Weigert 1991, 16).

contradiction and ambiguity. The media play an important role in this process, since they tend to support the dominant structures and interpretations (Gitlin 1979). Gusfield (1981, 53) noted in his analysis of public debates that although knowledge about a social phenomenon is often uncertain, inconsistent, and inaccurate at first, it is quickly "fashioned into a public system of certain and consistent knowledge in ways which heighten its believability and its dramatic impact." He called this phenomenon the "dramatic significance of fact." In their attempts to present coherent and forceful arguments, both the search activists and those who oppose open records have failed to understand experiences of adoption as rooted in conflicting cultural conceptions of the natural and the social aspects of kinship.

Adoption, Inequality, and the Law

THE ORIGINS OF THE SEALED
RECORDS CONTROVERSY

Adoptees view the policy of confidentiality as a euphemism for putting everyone's rights over their own, although as babies they had no say in the transaction.
—Betty Jean Lifton, "The Search"

Our society says that privacy is a really important thing, that people have a right to privacy. . . . It is not a presumption, it's what the United States Supreme Court says, among other things. It says that a person does have a right to privacy. And another person's need for information doesn't destroy your right to privacy.
—William Pierce, "Family Secret"

Few issues in American adoption policy have been as widely debated as the right of adoptees to have access to their original birth and adoption records without a court order. Search activists, mostly adoptees and birth mothers, have argued that the sealed records policy violates their constitutional rights, including their right to privacy.[1] Some have condemned the treatment of unwed mothers and illegitimate children as unfair; others have framed the debate in terms of a government attack on parental rights and the "natural family." Although search groups such as the Adoptees' Liberty Movement Association (ALMA) and Adoptees-in-Search have established their own

1. The Fourteenth Amendment prevents state intrusion in matters relating to procreation and family relationships (Simanek 1983, 126).

mutual-consent registries for adoptees and birth parents who wish to unite, search activists have so far rejected as insufficient this increasingly popular legal solution. According to Florence Fisher (1988), "mutual consent voluntary registries are an obstacle to adoptees' rights, not a step in the direction of more openness." The New York State Registry, for example, requires the consent of both of the biological parents as well as the consent of the adoptive parents. According to Fisher, some states also plan to require the searcher to submit to agency counseling in order to examine his or her motives for the search, even if information is gained through a "voluntary registry." All these measures serve to preserve confidentiality and restrict rather than facilitate adoptees' quest for genealogical knowledge.

With regard to the biological parents, the sealed records policy has contradictory consequences. The policy is intended to protect their constitutional right to anonymity or privacy, yet it also denies them any contact with children they have relinquished for adoption. Unlike adoptees who search, birth parents have not had the option of requesting a court order to open adoption records (Modell 1986, 648). Many adoption experts today acknowledge the importance of genealogical knowledge for the adoptee's identity concerns, but "the equivalent right of the birth parent to information about the adoptee is not accepted as legitimate and realistic" (Sachdev 1989, 121).[2] Like many other new social movements, the search movement first formed and articulated its agenda outside existing institutional channels of political expression. Although some child welfare professionals have been instrumental participants, the movement took form largely "outside, and in spite of, adoption agen-

2. Although the search movement comprises both adoptees and birth mothers (90 percent of the members of Concerned United Birthparents are women; Modell 1986, 647), this chapter focuses mainly on adoptees' effort to unseal their birth and adoption records.

cies" (Caplan 1990, 49). Jean Paton, an adoptee and a social worker, was the first to compile and report interviews with adoptees who questioned the conventional assumption in social work that detailed genealogical information should be kept confidential. Paton's book *The Adopted Break Silence* (1954) was an attempt to discuss adoption from the viewpoint of adoptees themselves and to challenge the tendency among practitioners to ignore the needs of adult adoptees. Although Paton's findings attracted little attention among social work professionals at the time, it provided support and motivation for many adoptees. In the 1950s, Paton organized the first search group, the Colorado-based Orphan Voyage (Sachdev 1989, 1).

The emergence of the search movement on a national level, however, had to wait for more favorable social conditions, the same conditions that propelled other minority and right-to-access movements of the 1970s. The civil rights movement provided the search movement, along with many other contemporary social movements, with ideological grounding, or what social movement theorists call a "master protest frame" (McAdam 1994, 49). The search movement is therefore

> essentially an outgrowth and an extension of the civil rights movement of the 1950s. . . . As society has developed conceptions of children's liberties, it has fostered a broadened perspective of the rights of the adopted person; specifically, it has encouraged the recognition of the rights of adopted children to fuller disclosure of information about themselves.

> The concern with searching for birth parents also has links to growing interest in ethnic origins and pride. Since the mid-1960s we have seen various ethnic groups demonstrate a growing fascination with their collective identities, increasingly

delving into their origins and family histories as they attempt to achieve closer touch with their "roots." As these interests in genealogical matters have been gathering momentum in society generally, their presence has created an environment very conducive to encouraging "the search." (Feigelman and Silverman 1983, 196).

Several events added to, and reflected, the momentum of the movement. In 1976, the Child Welfare League of America recommended for the first time that adoption agencies inform adopting parents that secrecy cannot be guaranteed (Sachdev 1989, 5). Since then, most major social work and child welfare journals have published debates on the disclosure of adoption files.[3] The notion of open adoption was first introduced to the social work community by a team of researchers in the mid-1970s (Baran, Pannor, and Sorosky 1976). In 1982, a group of adoption professionals known as the Ad Hoc Committee to Reevaluate Adoptive Placement Philosophy held its first national conference. Although the practice of open adoption was the primary theme, the conference prompted adoption professionals to reconsider the issues of "secrecy, anonymity, and [the] mystique surrounding the traditional adoptions" (Caplan 1990, 48).

As I have noted, an increasing number of adoption agencies today practice openness in adoption to varying degrees (see, e.g., Sorich and Siebert 1982), but most states and agencies have *not* unsealed their records. Both the National Committee for Adoption and the Child Welfare League of America have acknowledged some positive aspects of openness in adoption, but they have stopped short of advocating that previously sealed

3. *Public Welfare,* the journal of the American Public Welfare Association, published a special issue on this topic in 1979.

records be opened. Although most adoption practitioners and experts recognize that the issue of disclosure can no longer be avoided, many still stress the importance of flexibility in assessing their clients' needs rather than advocating their unconditional right to access (Amadio 1991, 29). Some have argued that the search activists represent only a minority of adoptees and that their arguments lack scientific legitimacy (Byrd 1988, 20).[4] The recent attempt by the National Conference of Commissioners on Uniform State Laws to create a Uniform Adoption Act reflects the persistence of the principle that records should be sealed unless all parties agree on disclosure (National Conference of Commissioners on Uniform State Laws 1994, 146).

As mentioned earlier, there are few reliable statistics on adoption in this country. The federal government stopped collecting adoption data in 1975, after funding for this purpose was withdrawn. In 1981 the number of adopted persons living in the United States was estimated at between five and nine million (Abernathy 1981, 2). The number of yearly adoptions rose from 72,000 in 1951 to a peak of 175,000 in 1970 and declined in the mid-1980s to approximately 100,000. Since 1971, unrelated adoptions have accounted for less than half of all adoptions (National Committee for Adoption [NCFA] 1989, 69).[5] Throughout the 1980s approximately 40 percent of these unrelated adoptions were handled by public agencies and under 30 percent by private agencies. Independent adoptions (that is, adoptions handled by lawyers rather than by public or private agencies) constitute an estimated 30 percent of unrelated

4. According to Cashman (1979, 19), for example, most adoptees primarily want to know why they were placed for adoption and do not wish to search for their birth mothers.
5. Contrary to popular image, in the United States most adoptees are biologically related to the adopter.

adoptions, although there are considerable variations among the states (NCFA 1989, 70).

In contrast to these relatively undisputed estimates, there is considerable disagreement regarding the number of searchers.[6] The defenders of closed records have maintained that "very few adoptees and birth parents seek to meet each other" (NCFA 1989, 5), but search activists point to the large and constantly growing number of search support groups. Particularly in the early stages of the search debate, the defenders of sealed records backed their arguments with statistical claims, sometimes making broad generalizations based on limited data. For example, one supporter of the status quo proclaimed that "less than 1 percent of a given population should [not] outweigh the rights of more than 99 percent," basing his argument on data collected in Scotland ten to twenty years earlier (Zeilinger 1979, 45). Another author based his support of continued confidentiality on a study carried out at a single adoption agency in Texas (Foster 1979, 36). Search activists have contended that all such estimates are meaningless, that "virtually all adoptees feel a sense of 'genealogical bewilderment'" (Lifton 1976, 15), and that a lack of interest in one's biological origins can be assumed to stem from conscious or unconscious psychological repression.

6. Constructionist studies of social problems have shown that statistics and "dark figures" are central to the process of claims making. Big numbers are more impressive than small ones, and official numbers are more convincing than unofficial ones (see Best 1987, 32). The media have their own reasons for preferring big, official numbers: large estimates add to the dramatic thrust of a story, and official statistics add to the air of journalistic objectivity. As in many other public debates, estimates have played a central role in the debate over the disclosure of birth records.

The Institutionalization of Adoption
in the United States

Although there has been no comprehensive historical or anthropological study of adoption, there is a fair amount of information available about the historical development of adoption and related parenting arrangements. Numerous historians and anthropologists have noted the importance of adoption in other countries, cultures, and epochs. Ancient patterns of adoption differ significantly from modern adoption in the United States and Europe, where the issue of child welfare has been pivotal (Goody 1969, 58). In the Roman republic, for example, adoption was intended to benefit the adopter rather than the adoptee in order to avoid extinction of the family and of family ancestral worship (Presser 1971, 446). The institution of adoption received considerable attention in the Babylonian code of Hammu-rabi (the oldest comprehensive set of written laws), as well as in the laws of China, Greece, and ancient Rome (Goody 1969, 55). In all these societies, adoption was intended primarily to provide the adopters with heirs.

Anthropological studies of adoption have focused in particular on Oceanic or Polynesian societies such as Hawaii, where adoption has been a frequent and casual type of family formation. According to a recent overview of anthropological research on adoption (Terrell and Modell 1994, 157, 159), it is potentially misleading to apply the single term *adoption* to diverse child-rearing arrangements in different cultures, but comparative anthropological research has the potential to problematize Western commonsense distinctions, such as kin and non-kin, and the assumed primacy of blood ties and genetic influences on human relations. Comparative research can illuminate the social construction of kinship and the ways the category of kinship is linked to other social categories, actions, and meanings. For instance, the relative informality of adoption in African-American communities has been explained by the greater flexibility of kinship terms and obligations in these communities (Stack 1975, 83).

In the United States, the institution of adoption developed quite differently from adoption in England, where it is based on common law, and from adoption in countries whose legal system is derived from Roman law. The latter, like the British, have been more reluctant to conceal consanguineal identity than is typical of North America (Chambers 1975, 122). The Massachusetts law of 1851 is considered the first modern adoption law, because, in contrast to Roman practice, it was designed to guarantee the welfare of children. During the Colonial period, the practice most closely approximating modern adoption was indenture, or "putting out" children (especially orphans) for service and apprenticeship.[7] By 1925, as noted in chapter 1, all forty-eight states had enacted some type of adoption legislation. In England, by contrast, the first Adoption Act was implemented in 1949. In fact, the social institution of adoption did not exist in English common law, an omission that has been explained by the unusually high regard for blood lineage, which supposedly made the practice difficult for the English to accept (Presser 1971, 448). The early institutionalization of adoption in the United States has been attributed to the "fluid social system, [the] underpopulated country, and [the] ideology that man was not simply born into his rank but created his own place in the world" (Shalev 1989, 38).

Initially, adoption in the United States did not involve the eradication of the adoptee's natal identity. Like current adoption regulations in most states, the nation's first sealed records

7. An examination of wills during the Colonial period, however, reveals that "colonists did indeed make a more specific and positive arrangement to make such children their own" (Kawashima 1981–82, 680, 688).

law, passed in 1917 in Minnesota, prohibited disclosure of identifying information to those concerned as well as to the general public. By the late 1940s, laws obliterating the adopted person's natal identity had become the rule rather than the exception, a development actively endorsed by the Child Welfare League of America (Aigner 1986, 7–8). Several factors contributed to this development, but most of them were in one way or another related to the new legal notion of the best interests of the child. Not all adoption institutions concurred with these secrecy standards; some used their discretionary power to continue to provide identifying and nonidentifying information to adoptees and their birth parents (Carp 1992). Nevertheless, until the 1980s, sealed records and closed adoptions remained the norm in American adoption practice. Paradoxically, several states continue to allow adoptees to inherit from their biological parents by intestacy despite sealed records laws (Beckman 1985, 353), and inheritance rights have occasionally justified the release of identifying information that otherwise would have remained sealed.

SEALED RECORDS AND THE
"BEST INTERESTS OF THE CHILD"

Most U.S. laws are based on English common law, but early adoption laws in this country were modeled after Roman law (Howe 1983, 175). Contrary to Roman practice, however, adoption in the United States was from the beginning explicitly intended to protect the welfare of parentless children—a principle referred to, ironically, as the "child-rescue aspect of modern adoption" (Benet 1976, 37). According to the search movement, the rhetoric of child welfare has instead served to conceal the self-interest of the adopters, the adoption agencies, and the government in the adoption process (e.g., Aigner 1986).

Regulations governing sealed records have also been explicitly justified as protecting the welfare of adopted children. Whereas critics of the policy have questioned this explanation, social workers and legislators originally justified the laws by arguing that they were needed to protect adoptees from the stigmatizing effects of illegitimacy, to ensure the stability of the adoptive family, and to safeguard the privacy of the birth parents. All these measures were purportedly intended to preserve the "integrity of the adoption process"—that is, to protect not only the adoptee's welfare but also the public's interest in avoiding the financial burden of providing for parentless children, controlling illegitimacy, and preserving the family unit (cf. Prager and Rothstein 1973).

Beginning with the 1917 Minnesota law, sealed records were gradually introduced throughout the country, making access to original birth records possible only by court order or after proof of "good cause." Just as English common law reflected the importance attributed to blood lineage in English society, so the American model of adoption reflected cultural assumptions about social mobility and the malleable nature of kinship and identity. On the other hand, the sealed records policy could also be interpreted as a safeguard against the power of blood ties (Bartholet 1993, 58–59).

The emergence since the Progressive Era of child welfare legislation and of the legal notion of the child's best interests has reflected a new perception of family privacy and parents' property rights in their child. Building on this premise, in the 1970s a law professor and two child psychoanalysts introduced the notion of "psychological parenthood" and argued that the continuity of psychological parenting is always in the child's best interest. According to Joseph Goldstein, Anna Freud, and Albert Solnit (1973), the importance of psychological parenting for the child's welfare overrules the biological parents' natural rights to the child. This principle does not favor the biological parents but assumes that the task of psychological parenting can be performed just as well by adoptive parents. Since the notion of the child's best interest was first used, in a 1881 Kansas Supreme Court ruling (Aigner 1986, 112), it has been challenged on the ground that what is best for children cannot be demonstrated or predicted on scientific grounds (Mnookin 1985, 16); that the notion of the child's best interest is "an amorphous generalization which varies from court to court" (Litt 1971, 135); and that this vague legal standard tends to ignore the special needs of minority children and families. This last argument was originally put forward by the National Association of Black Social Workers in their case against transracial adoption in the 1970s.

The Roman doctrine of *parens patriae* gave the state's representatives the right to determine the best interests of a child regardless of the parents' wishes.[8] Both the principle of parens patriae and the concept of the child's best interests are central to the debate over sealed records. Some search activists have viewed the doctrine of parens patriae as a major threat to the rights of both adoptees and their biological parents. According to this point of view, "the murky, dubious authority of *parens patriae*, and that largely speculative rumination from the behavioral sciences known as psychological parenthood" mask the government's attempt to erode the autonomy of the natural family (Aigner 1986, 140). To quote one critic: "When parents lose legal right over their children, it is not the children who gain more legal rights, it is the state" (Mandell 1973, 64).

Yet others have argued that the rights of children still tend

8. " 'Parens patriae,' literally 'parent of the country,' refers traditionally to the role of the state as sovereign and guardian of persons under legal disability" (*Black's Law Dictionary*, 5th ed.).

to be outweighed by "the proprietary if not the property rights of the biological parent(s)" (Schwartz 1983, 449). Anne Crane (1986, 661) claims that "although courts attempt to balance the interests of all the affected parties, they generally accord the greatest weight to the interests of the biological parents." Although legal standards in adoption have in some respects become more child-centered during the past decades (Mnookin and Weisberg 1989, 650), the trend in American legal opinion has been to limit the permissible grounds for governmental intervention in family life, restricting it primarily to the physical protection of children (cf. Dingwall, Eekelaar and Murray 1983, 225). This trend can be attributed to the far-reaching impact on the development of American family law of the doctrine of natural rights (of biological parents to the custody of their children), a doctrine that historically has been related to an emphasis on individual liberty and the limitation of governmental authority (Houlgate 1988, 20–21).

There are other reasons that the creation of sealed records laws cannot be explained solely in terms of a greater sensitivity to the needs of adoptees. As Viviana Zelizer (1985) has noted, the implementation of sealed records regulations marked a cultural shift from economically motivated adoptions to sentimental adoptions. The child welfare profession had its own reasons to support this transition. Until the 1920s most adoptions had been handled by doctors, lawyers, clergymen, or lay boards (Kirk 1985, 71). Because "one of the things adoption agencies claimed they could offer clients was the promise of greater confidentiality" (Gonyo and Watson 1979), the implementation of confidentiality in adoption legitimated the occupational niche of professional adoption workers. Hence, the monopolization of adoption work by social workers also served to enhance the status of the profession.

Nevertheless, references to the child's best interest continue to be central to the defense of sealed records laws and practices. Austin Foster (1979, 37), a leading advocate of confidential adoption, argues that

> infant adoption as it exists in England, Scotland, Germany, Finland, and France leaves the adopted child definitely in a second-class status. In contrast, the American pattern is based upon a daring legal fiction: our laws mean for the adopted child to become both in law and in fact a complete member of the family with precisely the same rights and privileges that would entail to a natural child, with the clear implication that this membership extends to all social, cultural, and emotional facets of that child's life. The American procedure makes the child a member of this family and of no other.
>
> It is my conviction that this has been as successful as it has been daring and that the American pattern of adoption has been far and away the most successful in the world.

According to Foster's line of reasoning, confidentiality or secrecy is functionally necessary for the adoption system to work—legally, socially, and psychologically. From the 1930s and 1940s to the 1970s, this view was largely supported by the social work profession. A 1976 study of attitudes toward the disclosure of adoption records among adoption agency workers found that over 80 percent of the respondents supported the principle of confidentiality on these grounds (Jones 1976, 29).

The Right to Know versus the Right to Privacy

Before the late 1960s, the need to resolve or balance the (in theory) conflicting interests of adoptees, birth parents, and adoptive parents stirred little debate in legal circles. In the 1970s and 1980s, however, new legal issues arose concerning the rights of unwed fathers, the adoption of children with special needs (in particular the issue of subsidized adoption), the practices of independent adoption and open adoption, and the sealed records controversy (Howe 1983, 185–93).

Legally, the search debate has focused on abolishing closed records laws, not on making adoption records available. Sealed records laws stipulate that all information about an adoptee's past (including the original birth certificate) must be filed and sealed when the adoptee has been issued a new birth certificate by the court. On the other hand, the records retained by the agency that handled the adoption are not usually covered by sealed records statutes. Most adoption agencies nonetheless treat them as though they were, mainly because they have agreed with the birth parents and adoptive parents to keep this information confidential. Yet it is uncertain to what extent adoption agencies have explicitly guaranteed anonymity to the adoptive parents and the biological parents and to what extent such promises are legally and morally binding (Jones 1976, 6). Search activists therefore have two ways of achieving their goal: they can attempt either to revoke existing laws or to transform adoption agency practices. Since the child-welfare-agency system tends to be more uniform than the state adoption laws, it has been suggested that adoption reform activists focus on changing social workers' guidelines instead of on reversing adoption laws (Kirk 1985, 145–56).

Different states have legislated different standards that must be met in order to open the records. The traditional legal procedure requires proof of "good cause." Because the notion of good cause has never been uniformly defined, it has been the focus of considerable debate. Some state courts, such as those of New

York and Washington, D.C. (Arndt 1986, 105, 118), have generally considered compelling psychological need a good enough cause for disclosure. But there are no clear guidelines for what constitutes "compelling need," and the courts' attempts to distinguish between "mere curiosity" and "compelling need" have increasingly led to battles involving psychiatric experts. In some states good cause can be demonstrated simply by suing to open the records (Tartanella 1982, 477); other state courts have not considered the mere desire to know good cause if the petitioner does not clearly demonstrate that this desire causes mental distress (Simanek 1983, 136). Some courts have categorically dismissed psychological need as a good cause and have even considered a compelling need for medical information insufficient cause for disclosure (Arndt 1986, 118). In general, courts have defined these concepts narrowly and have valued the biological parents' theoretical right to privacy over adoptees' right to know (Crane 1986, 661).

Since the constitutional issues relating to sealed records cases were first considered by a federal appellate court in 1979 (Simanek 1983, 127), there have been three main types of legal challenges to the constitutionality of closed-record statutes.[9] First, adoptees have argued that sealed records laws violate their right to privacy, and that the right to privacy includes the right to self-identity. Second, adoptees have appealed to equal-protection clauses, arguing that since adoptees constitute a "suspect class,"[10] it is the obligation of the state—not the adoptees—to prove compelling interest, in this case to support

9. For detailed overviews, see Simanek (1983, 126–33) and Crane (1986, 653–60).

10. If the state classifies and consequently treats certain categories of people differently from others, the state is obliged to justify its grounds for classification.

sealed records statutes. Third, adoptees have argued that sealed records laws violate their First Amendment right to receive information. So far, however, "state and federal courts have rejected every constitutional attack on sealed records statutes" (Crane 1986, 655).

A problem with the good cause standard is that "the real, present needs of the adopted are being 'balanced' against the theoretical needs of the natural parents" (Arndt 1986, 119). Some legal scholars have suggested that the needs of an adopted child are fundamentally different from those of an adopted adult and that the state's interest in supporting the autonomy of the adoptive family thus ceases when the adoptee reaches adulthood (Lawrence 1981, 371 n127). As Jean Paton noted, there has been a "tendency to be babyish in talking about adoption" and to pay less attention to the issues that concern adult adoptees (1954, 5).

The assumption that confidentiality serves the interests of adoptive and biological parents is problematic, since it is not clear how much privacy adoption agencies have promised parents and whether birth parents in fact wish to remain anonymous. In 1976 Mary Ann Jones found that 90 percent of the adoption agencies she surveyed claimed to have explicitly or implicitly guaranteed anonymity (6). According to search activists, however, anonymity has not been so much guaranteed as forced and requested by adoption workers (Modell 1986). Research also suggests that a majority of adoptive parents favor the disclosure of identifying information (Feigelman and Silverman 1986; Sachdev 1989, 78). In addition, although some proponents of anonymity in the adoption process continue to argue that the birth mother's right to privacy is essential to her decision to surrender her child for adoption (Tartanella 1982, 458), the growing number of open adoptions in the United States challenges the traditional contention that openness inhibits a mother's adoption decision. Yet opponents of open records have maintained that adoptees' interests do not overrule the biological parents' theoretical right to privacy and that "there are too many persons who could be too easily hurt to permit totally unfettered access to court records" (Fox 1979, 51).

An increasingly preferred solution to the dilemma of balancing the interests of the state and the members of the adoptive triangle is the establishment of mutual-consent adoption registries. By 1993, approximately twenty states had established "passive" registries, and seventeen others had adopted some type of "confidential intermediary" approach (Hollinger 1993, 52). The mutual-consent registries require consent from both the adoptee and the birth parent(s) in order for identifying information to be released. Not surprisingly, some legal experts have regarded mutual-consent registries as the only "truly voluntary option" for birth parents (Fay 1987, 681), whereas other experts argue that the only fair solution would be to assume consent and release identifying information to adoptees unless the birth parents request otherwise (Arndt 1986, 122). Search activists have in general described these registries as insufficient, because the system prioritizes confidentiality and ultimately hinges on the birth parents' voluntary and positive response (Fisher 1988). These issues continue to be actively debated by activists, social workers, legal scholars, and those in the media. In sum, adoptees have been more successful in broadening the definition of "good cause" (with the help of expert psychiatric testimony) than in challenging the constitutionality of sealed records laws. The most important argument has concerned adoptees' psychological need for information about the birth parents, or the assumption that "knowledge of one's heritage is a necessary part of identity formation" (Sachdev 1989, 12). This aspect of the controversy is most interesting from a sociological point of view, since it involves the social definitions of the blood relation, identity, and kinship.

Although courts have unanimously rejected "mere curiosity" as a cause for releasing identifying information, a "compelling psychological need" has in some instances warranted a release of information (Crane 1986, 661). However, even if courts have tried to distinguish mere curiosity from compelling need on an individual basis, cases in which an adoptee has been granted access to identifying information on the basis of psychological need have often been supported by psychological theories and viewpoints that portray such needs as universally present, albeit sometimes latent, in all adoptees. As one legal scholar summarized the argument, "There is evidence to support the theory that to have a healthy and productive life, the development of one's personal identity is important. A corollary would be that if the adoptee is denied access to the identity of his natural parents, his own identity formation may be hindered" (Manson 1979, 797 n45; see also Arndt 1986, 109).

To grant adoptees access to identifying information on the basis of psychological need thus simultaneously undermines the distinction between mere curiosity and real need and challenges the very existence of the good cause requirement. Although the good cause requirement assumes that the need to have access to identifying information is neither normal nor universal, the evidence used to prove the existence of a compelling psychological need assumes that genealogical curiosity is a normal and desirable developmental need.

In addition, the effort to unlock adoption files has so far depended largely on the willingness of the courts to reinscribe assumptions of biological determinism. By stressing genetic elements at the expense of the social construction of identity, some courts have reinforced the popular assumption that genes rather than social relationships form families and identities (cf. Nelkin and Lindee 1995). Moreover, by framing the issue in terms of psychological needs while ignoring the underlying institutional and cultural conflicts of adoption, the sealed records debate has tended to mask the common roots of the problems of adoptees, their birth parents, and their adoptive parents.

ADOPTION AND INEQUALITY

Search activists and other critics of the American adoption system have argued that the institution mirrors and perpetuates inequalities of class, race, and gender in the larger society. It has been argued that adoption not only relieves the state of the burden of providing for parentless children but also provides the ruling group (Benet 1976, 70) with a means of regulating the reproductive behavior of the poor, upholding the sanctity of the conjugal family, and securing the orderly transfer of property.

Even though adoption agencies do not require a minimum income for adoptive parents, the income of those who do end up adopting successfully is usually well above the average (Bachrach et al. 1990). Betty Reid Mandell (1973, 2) argued in her analysis of foster care and adoption in the United States that the problems of both the adoption and the foster care systems "flow out of the problems of the larger society" and that the adoption system relies upon and reinforces class domination: "To obtain children, the middle and the upper classes are more likely than the working and lower classes to turn to adoption agencies rather than to relatives and informal community contacts. The adopted children come not only from strangers, but frequently from poor strangers and from unmarried mothers, who have a stigmatized social status" (29).

Mary Kathleen Benet (1976, 70) describes modern adoption as a system "created by, and intended to serve the white ruling group." The sealed records policy in particular has been criticized for putting the adopters' interests first and for expressing the adopters' fear of the birth parents and a "class prejudice against the poor" (Shalev 1989, 39). Similar criticisms have been directed against intercountry and transracial adoptions. John Triseliotis (1993, 119–37) has commented that the moral arguments favoring or opposing intercountry adoption oscillate between ecumenical humanitarianism and exploitation. Proponents of international adoption have stressed the moral responsibility to provide homes for all parentless children; critics have claimed that it exploits poor women and children politically and economically in developing countries (Herrman and Kasper 1992; Fieweger 1991).

The search for ethnic roots among transracial adoptees epitomizes the importance of self-identity. In contrast to other adoption topics, the issue of transracial adoption has received some attention from sociologists (Kirk 1985, 3). Opponents and supporters continue to debate whether transracial adoptions violate the identity needs of minority children. Critics have argued that adoption has served the white community predominately and that not enough effort has been made to attract adopters from other ethnic groups (cf. Hayes 1993). Although the underrepresentation of African-American and other minority adopters has in part been explained by their preference for informal adoptions, adoption agencies have clearly played an active role in excluding adopters on the basis of economic resources and thus implicitly on the basis of race (Chimezie 1975). Race and class, along with gender, age, family structure, and sexual preference, are major structuring principles in the American adoption system.

Furthermore, like all Western adoption systems, adoption in the United States has been crucially shaped by the "twin stigmata of infertility and illegitimacy." According to Erica

Haimes and Noel Timms (1985), adoption in Great Britain "has also been associated with secrecy, which has served to preserve certain social standards of morality and normality, as well as, within certain constraints, the reputations of individuals" (77). Although most adoption experts today agree that information about one's adoption should not be hidden from the adoptee, opponents of adoption reform have continued to characterize institutionalized secrecy or sealed records as serving the best interests of all parties involved. Search activists, on the other hand, have argued that institutionalized secrecy reinforces rather than remedies stigmatization and shame.

Feminist scholars have contended that adoption laws and practices reflect the norms and power structures of a male-dominated gender order and that the social control aspect of adoption has most punitively affected the lives of unwed birth mothers. Like welfare policies in general, adoption has been used as a vehicle for controlling women's behavior and sexuality and for perpetuating the patriarchal family.[11] According to Linda Gordon (1985), welfare policies aimed at helping the "neglected children" of single mothers have been shaped by a bias against unwed single mothers, who have violated patriarchal ideals of family life. Although legislatures since the Progressive Era have in most respects removed the legal differences between illegitimate children and children born to married couples, in reality mothers of illegitimate children have not been treated like other single mothers by social service agencies (Mason 1994, 99).

Historical studies of attitudes toward illegitimacy in the

11. Studies of community attitudes toward adoption have revealed that at least until the mid-1960s negative images were "most closely associated with disparaging attitudes toward illegitimacy and toward the meanings of motherhood" (Kirk 1985, 23). For a more in-depth feminist discussion, see chap. 6.

United States since the late nineteenth century have reflected a changing view of the white unwed mother—from a fallen woman to be saved to a sexual delinquent to be controlled to a neurotic girl to be cured (Kunzel 1993). For unwed mothers of color, different rules and assumptions have applied. Rather than explaining illegitimacy as the neurotic symptom or the unresolved psychic conflict of an individual (see chap. 3), child welfare professionals have attributed out-of-wedlock pregnancies among women of color to a general cultural pathology (Solinger 1994). Carmel Shalev (1989, 38) has argued that the American institutionalization of adoption in the mid-nineteenth century came about as "a result of social concern for the plight of the illegitimate child and the political pressure of middle-class childless couples." The interest of middle-class couples in adoption was prompted by "the cult of romanticized motherhood" and family life, which also supported the passage of sealed records laws that completely obscured the adoptee's biological origins.

Until the 1980s, the psychological consequences of relinquishment for the birth mother were seldom researched or explored in adoption practice. Instead, adoption experts viewed the adoption as a possibility for the birth mother to start her life over, without any "guilt and confusion" (Foster 1979, 37). In contrast, feminist critics have argued that by denying the birth mother any contact with the adopted child, the sealed records policy retained some of the punitive social control characteristics of earlier laws affecting the poor (Shalev 1989, 11). Yet feminist scholars and critics have so far paradoxically neglected to analyze the problematic social position of adoptive mothers from a gender perspective. Gender domination has been considered crucial for understanding the situation of birth mothers, whereas the situation of adoptive mothers has been seen as determined primarily by social class. As noted in the introduction, the failure to problematize the situation of adoptive mothers is perhaps a reflection of the recent biocentric, and at times essentialist, turn in feminist thinking and scholarship, a perspective that has been shared by many search activists.

FAMILY IDEOLOGY AND ADOPTION EXPERTISE

Those who argue that adoption laws and practices reflect inequalities in the wider society have so far not provided a nuanced explanation of the role of adoption expertise in perpetuating these inequalities. According to the social control thesis, social policies serve to control individuals and groups who threaten the status quo or the interests of powerful social groups. For example, in his analysis of family policy in nineteenth-century France, Jacques Donzelot (1978) explored the emerging surveillance of the family through the absorption of child welfare philanthropy by the state. In contrast to most proponents of the social control thesis, however, Donzelot downplayed "the existence of a hierarchy of determinate power relations" and underscored the ambiguous and contradictory nature and consequences of governmental policies. Donzelot located the source of this ambiguity and tension in the "variety of alliances between the state, moralizing philanthropy, promotional feminism, the professions, relational counsellors, and family members" (see Elliot 1986, 457).

From this theoretical perspective, the passing of sealed records laws in the United States in the early twentieth century appears not simply as a facade for state-sanctioned attempts by the power elite to control and regulate women's reproductive behavior and provide rich people with babies. Inequalities in adoption are the outcome of a much more complex set of social forces that includes society's ambiguous beliefs about the nature of kinship and the conflicting interests of several groups. First, one cannot deny that American legislators over the past century have expanded their definitions of children's rights. Inequalities in the adoption system are partly unintended effects of policies aimed to advance the best interests of children, which reflect profound changes (even if they are limited and selective) in society's attitude toward child welfare. This recognition of children's rights does not, however, exclude the possibility that policies and practices aimed at advancing children's interests, such as the legal standard of the child's best interest, have de facto perpetuated existing social patterns of domination. As Anthony Giddens (1984) has pointed out, it is precisely in the unintended consequences of actions that the constraining impact of social structures becomes most clearly discernible.

Second, although adoption practices in reality have clearly worked in favor of privileged individuals (in terms of gender, class, and race), adoption laws and practices also reflect cultural beliefs about the significance of blood ties that surpass these divisions. Although these beliefs may serve the interests of some groups more than others, they cannot be reduced to these social divisions: the analyses of adoption along class lines especially have so far been too crude. As I show in chapter 3, many adoption experts have tended to view adoptive parents as inherently inferior and lacking despite their economic privilege. Researchers have in particular reinforced essentialist and normative images of femininity and motherhood. As noted, the sealed records policy also paradoxically assumes that blood relations *are* important enough to threaten the stability of the adoptive family.

Third, the tendency to explain problems in the adoptive family in terms of individual shortcomings or medical terms, while overlooking disparaging social attitudes and inconsistent adoption practices that complicate adoptive family life, has been further reinforced by the collective goal of social workers to gain professional prestige. The development of the adoption system is intricately intertwined with the development of social work and the endorsement by social workers of an individualistic, psychomedical model of adoptive family relations. Moreover, since professional adoption agencies could claim that only they were able to guarantee confidentiality in adoption, sealed records regulations enabled social workers to both monopolize adoption work and advance their own professional project (see Larson 1977).

Studies of American family ideology have revealed the primacy of the blood relation in definitions of kinship and the family. In *American Kinship*, David Schneider (1980) noted that kinship bonds in American society are defined exclusively in terms of blood ties. From a more critical point of view, Jon Bernardes (1985, 284) observed not only that blood is considered the proper basis for family formation but that other forms of family formation and bonding consequently tend to be regarded as pathological and unworkable. And as Dorothy Nelkin and Susan Lindee (1995) argue, this genetic or molecular definition of kinship and family has become even more prominent in the popular and scientific culture of the 1990s.

Yet opposing themes are not absent from the public debate on adoption. The sealed records controversy is a debate between two opposing conceptions of kinship, one emphasizing the biological nature of kinship and the other emphasizing the primacy of social bonds. In her anthropological study of the activist group Concerned United Birthparents, Judith Modell (1986) argued that the group exposes a central tension in American kinship ideology, that of the relative importance of biological bonds and social parenting: Is the basis of parenthood primarily natural or social? This tension typifies not only CUB rhetoric but the search controversy as a whole. The search issue has captured the public's attention because it is a symbolic battleground for conflicting views on the nature of the family. The search debate continues a long tradition of thinking about kinship and identity that is, if not peculiar to, at least profoundly embedded in the ideological and cultural structure of American society. Although the idea that adoptees are entitled access to genealogical information is relatively novel in the history of American adoption, the arguments and the symbolism used to legitimate access are not.

3

Adoption Research

TRENDS AND PERSPECTIVES

Adoption agency practices have undergone several significant changes since adoption first came to be regarded as a welfare service during the Progressive Era. The emphasis on heredity and the importance of testing adopted children for possible genetic defects, which dominated the adoption process during this period, was replaced in the 1940s by a focus on the prospective adopters' aptitude for parenting. This conversion to psychodynamic theory and a new emphasis on parenting skills and environmental influences on child development significantly reformed the field, although the consideration of genetic factors was never completely abandoned. These changes in adoption practice, however, did not reflect solely an increasing concern for the adoptee; they also were the result of an increasing number of applicants for adoptive parenthood and of social workers' collective pursuit of professional prestige. Although prospective adoptive parents were subjected to increasing scrutiny by adoption agencies, the promise of confidentiality, as we have seen, was an added incentive for them to choose agency services over independently arranged adoptions (Reitz and Watson 1992, 236).

Adoption agencies in the post–World War II era have downplayed the importance of heredity; yet definitions of kinship and attitudes toward adoption in society at large have never ceased to emphasize the blood relation. As H. David Kirk noted in his classic study *Shared Fate* (1964, 23), adoption professionals continued in the 1950s to give adoptive parents the message that genetic factors were important. Today, for instance, the practice of "matching" the adopters' and the adoptee's personalities remains central to the adoption process (Modell 1994, 43).

In the 1990s, genetic definitions of kinship and identity have become even more common in popular and scientific culture (Nelkin and Lindee 1995, 58–78). The concept of genetics influencing behavior also appears to have gained currency among adoption advocates. The authors of a recent book on reforms in the adoption system, for example, argue that nature is a stronger behavioral influence than nurture and applaud new psychological screening methods that make reliable psychological evaluation possible (McKelvey and Stevens 1994, 135). According to these authors, it is important that adoptive parents accept their children's inherited traits and not try to change them.

In this chapter I argue that despite social workers' tendency to emphasize the importance of environmental influences on child development and identity (Cominos 1971), their definition of "environmental influences" has remained narrow and partial. Adoption research, and presumably, therefore, also adoption practice, has endorsed a psychopathological model of adoption that explains problems in adoptive families in narrow individualistic and biological terms (cf. Haimes and Timms 1985, 80–81). Although the recent clinical interest in issues surrounding the search for biological relatives in some respects indicates a major change in American adoption practice, the underlying theoretical perspectives that inform adoption research continue to depict adoptive families as, at least potentially, deviant and pathological.

The Psychopathological Model

The link between adoption and emotional disturbance has intrigued psychiatrists, social workers, and other mental health professionals at least since the 1940s, and the search for pathological symptoms among adoptees has generated more than 150 studies over the past fifty years (Howard 1990). Most such studies have asserted that adoptees are "different" and that this "difference" can ultimately be attributed to the lack of a biological bond between the adoptee and the adoptive parents (Marquis and Detweiler 1985). Some researchers have focused on the effects of early maternal deprivation on the adoptee, the lack of genealogical knowledge, and various hereditary factors; others have emphasized the impact of psychodynamics in the adoptive family, especially parental attitudes and behaviors (Hajal and Rosenberg 1991). Most researchers have implied that the absence of blood relations in itself renders adoption pathogenic.

The extent to which adoptees suffer from negative personality traits or mental disorders has also been the subject of considerable dispute. Some recent studies indicate that adoptees as a group are at lower risk of suffering from negative personality characteristics such as poor self-image, insecurity, and lack of control than are persons raised by their biological parents (Benson, Sharma, and Roehlkepartain 1994; Marquis and Detweiler 1985) and that adoption itself should not be seen as pathogenic (Brinich and Brinich 1982). Yet most researchers have maintained that adoptees are at greater risk of suffering from psychiatric disorders (e.g., LeVine and Sallee 1990; Berry 1992). Marshall Schechter (1960) presented particularly influential data indicating an extreme overrepresentation of adopted children in his psychiatric clinic. These findings were soon challenged on methodological grounds by several authors (e.g., Kadushin 1966; Simon and Senturia 1966; Reece and Levin 1968), but most researchers have nevertheless agreed with the theoretical perspectives that inform Schechter's work.[1] The psychopathology of adoption has also received considerable attention in the mass media.

The purpose of this chapter is not to assess whether adoptees are in fact more prone to suffer from emotional problems than nonadopted individuals.[2] Rather, it is to describe and analyze the hidden normative assumptions that have guided research on mental health and adoption, from Helene Deutsch's (1945) pioneering work on infertile adoptive mothers and unmarried birth mothers to David Kirschner's recent definition of the "adopted child syndrome" as a synopsis of antisocial behaviors common among adoptees (Kirschner 1992; Kirschner and Nagel 1988). I claim that there has been a strong tendency in adoption research to decontextualize the research subjects' experiences and consequently to define adoptive kinship as intrinsically different, defective, and pathogenic from blood relations. I emphasize, however, that my analysis focuses on major research trends: not all adoption researchers espouse a psychopathological model of adoption. Some recent multidimensional

1. For example, Menlove (1965); Offord, Laponte, and Cross (1969); Ripple (1968); and Work and Anderson (1971). Kirk, Jonassohn, and Fish (1966) are notable exceptions.

2. Research findings remain contradictory, although discrepancies in findings are at least partly due to different research methodologies both with regard to sample selection and analytical approach. Many studies of adoption and mental health have also been based on self-selected samples and have typically focused on adopted children rather than on adult adoptees (cf. Brinich and Brinich 1982; Brodzinsky 1993). I do not deny that the causes or symptoms of adoptees' mental health problems differ from the causes and symptoms found among nonadopted persons or that the adoptive family environment affects the adoptees' well-being and personality development.

contributions to the clinical literature account for environmental variables as well (e.g., D. M. Brodzinsky 1990).

Kirk's *Shared Fate: A Theory of Adoption and Mental Health* (1964) is probably the most significant scholarly attempt to approach the issue of adoption and mental health from a cultural or sociological perspective, and I shall therefore review references to this work in the subsequent adoption literature. In conclusion I present an alternative sociopsychological model of adoption research that recognizes the impact of social stigmatization on the experiences and behavior of adoptees and adoptive parents. I begin, however, with a brief historical overview of the development of American adoption practice in light of the professionalization of social work.

ADOPTION AND THE PROFESSIONALIZATION OF SOCIAL WORK

Adoption professionals have argued that the practice of adoption mirrors societal needs and attitudes and that adoption agencies hence are "creatures of the public" (Reid 1957, 22; Dukette 1984).[3] The knowledge base of adoption practice, however, has also been shaped by the scientific orientation and professionalization of social work.[4] As Kirk wrote, "If a group seeks

3. This view of the mandate given to social work is largely compatible with the functionalist theory of professions, which was pervasive in the sociological literature of professions in the 1950s and 1960s. According to this perspective, the emergence of new areas of knowledge and the application of this knowledge reflect society's need for these types of knowledge and expertise.

4. In the 1970s, a new (so-called neo-Weberian) approach to the study of professions emerged, which focused on the process of professionalization, or the promotion and strategies of knowledge-based groups (Larson 1977). In contrast to functionalist theories, neo-Weberian theories of pro-

a monopoly of practice through public licensing, it must of necessity claim special competence" (1964, 22). In the United States, evidence for the scientific basis of child welfare work may have been particularly important for the professionalization of social workers because of the relative underdevelopment of other areas of social welfare. Until the 1970s, adoption work was in fact characterized by considerable professional prestige (Kirk 1985, 95).

The scientification or, as some commentators have suggested, the masculinization of social work has been well documented. In brief, efforts to professionalize social work began after the Civil War, prompted by "scientific philanthropists" who aimed to make charity "a matter of the head as well as of the heart" (Dressel 1987, 300). Particularly consequential in this respect was a speech by Abraham Flexner in 1915, in which he repudiated social workers' claim to professionalism (Austin 1983; Franklin 1986). Comparing social work and medicine, Flexner argued that social work could best be characterized as a "mediating activity" rather than "an original agency." Flexner's prescriptions, David Austin (1983, 373) argues, "contributed to skewing the development of social work toward a medical model." In an attempt to make social work more scientific, the early clinical theories were pervaded by medical metaphors, and some policymakers suggested that social problems be approached from a medical point of view (Goldstein 1990, 34).[5]

---

fessionalization focus on the role of self-interest in the production and promotion of expertise.

5. As neo-Weberian scholars have noted, claims to esoteric knowledge of scientific rationality are central to the process whereby a field can gain professional status. Like members of other so-called helping professions, social workers and child welfare workers are concerned primarily with concrete solutions to individual cases, and the neglect of the social context in adoption expertise might, therefore, not seem surprising. Yet, as Freid-

It is against this background that one can understand the claims for scientific rationality that were salient in the adoption field between the 1920s and the 1940s. Before the 1920s, child placements or adoptions were handled primarily by lay representatives or by private philanthropic organizations (see, e.g., Abbott 1937, 128–50). Since then, professional social work organizations have attempted to limit child-placement services to licensed agencies to prove that they had the training and expertise necessary to handle adoptions better than lay boards and independent adoption practitioners. By contrasting the common-sense and intuitive decision making of lay practitioners with the scientific rationality of professional child welfare workers, social workers both monopolized adoption work and advanced their broader professional project. In an article entitled "Adoption of Illegitimate Children: The Peril in Ignorance," the secretary of the Michigan Children's Aid Society expressed the following views: "Social workers must adopt a saner policy. Call it a more scientific method. . . . We must carry back into every last case that we handle the high standards of case work, the scientific fact-finding and interpreting which we discuss in conferences and adopt by unanimous vote" (Stoneman 1926, 8).

According to Arnold Gesell (1927, 2), a member of the Child Welfare League of America and an advocate of testing the prospective adoptee's mental potential, "The task of child adoption is indeed so complicated that it cannot be entrusted to sheer impulse or to unassisted common sense. . . . We should take nothing for granted, but appraise these [developmental] potentialities as judiciously as possible, through appropriate diagnos-

---

son (1970) has pointed out with regard to the clinical mentality of medical practitioners, the individualism that distinguishes the clinical mind is not solely dependent on the nature of medical work but is also "reinforced by social elements that have little to do with the work itself" (172). One such social element is the collective pursuit of professional power and prestige.

tic methods. . . . Clinical safeguards cannot solve all the problems of child adoption, but they can make them both more scientific and humane."

Until the 1950s, social workers placed greater emphasis on the study and screening of the child than on the characteristics and qualifications of the applicant couple (Lawder et al. 1969, 6).[6] Although adoption agencies in earlier decades often refused to place a child in an adoptive home before an assessment could be made of the child's possible genetic defects, in the mid-1940s this practice was to some extent replaced by equally rigorous methods of screening the prospective adoptive parents. The assessment of adopters' "adoption readiness" continues to be central to adoption practice, and "resolution of infertility" is still regarded as the most important precondition for their readiness to adopt (Daly 1990).

Since the 1950s, the training of most adoption workers has been carried out within the framework of psychodynamic theory (Kirk 1985, 84–97). Although in 1950 most unrelated adoptions were still independently arranged (Stolley 1993, 30), the professional guidelines described in the clinical literature set the parameters for the nation's adoption policy. With psychoanalysis having become an exclusively medical enterprise in the United States in the early decades of the century, adoption workers were eager to employ Freudian models of explanation.[7] The psychomedical method was well suited to enhance the professional image of social work. In addition, the use of psychody-

6. As Zelizer (1985, 194) has noted, however, as early as the 1920s the sentimentalization of adoption may have been enhanced by environmental theories of development. Yet, prior to the 1940s, few adoption agencies used psychodynamic methods to assess or work with adoption applicants.

7. That is, psychoanalysis was translated into a scientific/medical method whereby patients or clients could be observed "through the spectacles of abstraction." See Bettelheim (1985, 5-6).

namic theories in assessing the suitability of prospective adoptive parents was prompted by the practical need of adoption agencies to select adopters. Because of the threefold increase in legal adoptions that occurred between 1934 and 1944 (Zelizer 1985, 169–207), resulting from the cultural trend toward the sentimentalization of childhood, adoption agencies recognized the need to revise their selection requirements.[8]

From the very beginning, the psychomedical approach to adoption was characterized by a narrow focus on individual pathology. This was the case in Schechter's article of 1960, in which he reported a 100-to-1 overrepresentation of adopted children in his psychiatric clinic. His findings were criticized by several researchers, who argued that self-selected clinical populations cannot provide the basis for general assessments of adoption and mental health. They also noted that adoptive parents might be exceptionally prone to make use of mental health facilities (Kirk, Jonassohn, and Fish 1966; Brodzinsky 1993). Nonetheless, Schechter's explanations for the perceived overrepresentation have remained largely unchallenged. Following Freud's theory of the family romance, he argued that adoptees were unable to overcome the bad parent/good parent split and that they were narcissistically injured by the abandonment of their biological parents. He also noted defensive feelings and emotional problems among the adoptive parents, especially the adoptive mothers, which he thought caused or contributed to the adoptee's problems. However, by attributing psychiatric

8. As Zelizer (1985, 174) notes, as late as 1910 birth mothers were charged with a "surrender fee" by baby farmers who took on their children. The sale value of surrendered babies could be as low as twenty-five cents. By the 1930s, the sentimentalization of adoption had created an unprecedented demand for white babies. It also accounted for the fact that adoptees in America no longer had economic value but were treated instead as emotional investments.

symptoms among adoptees to the failure of adoptive parents in general and adoptive mothers in particular to adjust and accept their (presumed) infertility, Schechter launched a tradition of research that emphasizes individual pathology but obscures the cultural influence of stigmatization. Until the 1970s, moreover, virtually all research on adoption focused on the adoptive family, while the biological parents figured merely as genetic ghosts.

Research on Birth Mothers

As I noted in chapter 2, like welfare policies in general (see, e.g., Carby 1992; Maher 1992; Phoenix and Woollett 1991), adoption has been seen as a vehicle for controlling women's behavior and sexuality and for perpetuating the patriarchal family (Chesler 1989; Rothman 1989; Shalev 1989).[9] The mechanisms for controlling women's behavior have, however, been crucially differentiated according to race. Whereas white unwed mothers in the 1930s were expected to keep their "children of sin" (Solinger 1994, 288), after World War II the new market for babies prompted adoption workers to press the mother to relinquish her child for adoption. This task was supported by the new professional interest in Freudian psychodynamic theory. However, though out-of-wedlock pregnancies among white women were interpreted as symptoms of neurosis and unresolved psychic conflicts, child welfare professionals explained such pregnancies among women of color in terms of cultural rather than individual pathology (Kunzel 1993; Solinger 1994). Unlike white

9. As Johnson (1992, 19) has observed, from a Foucauldian perspective the modern helping professions are part of the "socio-technical devices through which the means and even the ends of government are articulated." In modern societies, professional expertise has thus become a prerequisite for the exercise of political power.

birth mothers, black women were not encouraged to relinquish their children for adoption. As Rickie Solinger (1992, 6-7, 154) notes, black women and their babies were not valued as market commodities.

In her classic Freudian work *The Psychology of Women* (1945), Helene Deutsch mapped the psychopathology of both infertile women and single mothers and described out-of-wedlock pregnancy as a masochistic act or a form of rebellion. Some contemporary clinical theorists have continued to argue that relinquishment is always in the unwed mother's best interest, because the motives for the unwanted pregnancy are immature or spurred by "unconscious needs" (Kraft et al. 1985). Writing in *The Encyclopedia of Mental Health*, Viola Bernard (1963, 73-74) argued that "in most instances, an unwed mother can ensure a healthier future for her baby through adoption." According to such views, unmarried white women who wanted to keep their babies were by definition immature, selfish, and unsuited for motherhood (Solinger 1992, 155). Despite the increasing power and say of birth mothers in the adoption process and the growing number of open adoptions in the United States (see, e.g., Melina and Rozia 1993), this attitude has apparently continued to influence adoption practice to some extent. Even in the 1980s, Linda Burgess (1981) continued to argue that "many mothers keep their babies for neurotic and vindictive reasons which they do not fully understand."

Of the three groups most intimately affected by adoption— adoptees, adoptive parents, and birth parents—the last has traditionally received the least attention. Until recently, research on birth mothers was heavily biased toward issues of relinquishment, especially factors influencing the decision to relinquish, though the effects of that relinquishment on the birth mother have been neglected (Curtis 1990). Compared to the relatively constant interest in issues of adoption and mental health, few studies before 1980 explored the emotional meaning of adoption for mothers who made the decision to give their children up (A. Brodzinsky 1990, 295–315). The recent argument by The National Committee for Adoption (1989, 148) that adoption tends to have mostly positive effects for the birth mother echoes a statement made thirty years earlier by the director of the Child Welfare League of America that adoption agencies have the responsibility to "point out to the unmarried mother the extreme difficulty, if she remains unmarried, of raising her child successfully in our culture without damage to the child and herself" (Reid 1957, 27).

The psychological issues of grief and survival addressed by Suzanne Arms (1990) in her book based on interviews with birth mothers are now discussed in most professional guides to adoption work (e.g., Kadushin and Martin 1988). Still, empirical research on relinquishment in the United States has emphasized the risks involved in becoming an unwed mother, supported an optimistic view of relinquishment, and stressed the social benefits of adoption (Curtis 1990, 245). Researchers have argued that because teenage pregnancies have serious economic and psychosocial consequences for the mothers, it is the social worker's professional duty to press for relinquishment. Yet, by presenting adoption as a solution to the dangers of teenage pregnancy and unwed motherhood, dangers that are seen as *inherent* in unwed motherhood, one can ignore the larger social context—the unavailability of contraceptives and the lack of prenatal care, health care, and welfare benefits. The tendency to attribute the economic hardships faced by single mothers to their "unweddedness" disguises the lack of state support for children. The emphasis on the positive effects of relinquishment among minority mothers is particularly misleading, since children of color stand a much lesser chance of being adopted than do white infants (Bowen 1987/1988). Research on relinquishment thus reinforces inequalities based on class and race and is consequently intrinsically political in nature. By depicting the problems of single mothers as dangers inherent to unwed motherhood instead of as issues stemming from an unequal distribution of resources, adoption research has also reinforced racial and class inequalities *among* women.

When the literature on adoption has treated the subject of birth parents, it has focused primarily on the birth mother and paid little attention to the birth father (Sachdev 1991). The terms *birth parent* or *biological parent* have sometimes been used interchangeably with *birth mother* or *biological mother*. Research on genetic resemblances between adoptees and their biological parents has tended to include information only about the birth mother, though the results have been presented as if both biological parents had been included in the study (e.g., Horn 1983). Although misleading references to the biological parents could be interpreted as an attempt to avoid excluding the biological father from adoption theory and practice, this convention in fact obscures the omission of birth fathers in adoption research. By the same token, failure to recognize that *birth parent* often stands for *birth mother* obscures the significance of gender in the adoption process and in society at large. Yet, while feminist commentators have considered gender domination crucial for understanding the situation of birth mothers, they have largely failed to analyze the problematic social position of adoptive mothers from a gender perspective.

The Psychopathology of Adoptive Motherhood

The first psychodynamic theories to appear in the adoption literature, published in the mid-1940s, were concerned with the negative psychological effect of childlessness on an adoptive mother's capacity to give her adopted child maternal love.

This approach reflected the general belief among mental health professionals during this period that mothering is based on instinct and that children's (and society's) problems stem from the mother's personality or misguided subconscious urges (Eyer 1992, 110–16). Deutsch (1945, 397) was particularly influential in developing this line of theorizing and wrote of "the sterile woman['s ability to] overcome the narcissistic mortification of her inferiority as a woman to such an extent that she is willing to give the child, as object, full maternal love." This approach identified women's presumed inability to conceive as the primary cause of the adoptee's psychological problems. Similarly, Schechter (1960, 48) characterized the adoptee "as a constant reminder of [the adoptive mother's] barrenness."

Another telling example of this view was presented by Povl Toussieng (1962, 65), who argued that "children who have been adopted at an early age and/or who have not been exposed to psychological traumatization before adoption seem to be more prone to emotional disturbances and personality disorders than nonadopted children. It is hard to explain these difficulties merely on the basis of the children's awareness of being adopted. It seems much more feasible to think of an unconscious and unresolved aversion towards parenthood in one or both adoptive parents, particularly the mother, as the original cause of the child's disturbance."

In a slightly different vein, Simon and Senturia (1966) and Reece and Levin (1968) argued that the emotional disturbances of adoptees stem from the hostility that develops between the adoptive parents as a result of their childless state; this hostility is then projected onto the adopted child. Recent studies have explained adoptees' mental health problems primarily in terms of the adoptive parents' lack of self-acceptance (DiGiulio 1988), unrealistic expectations (Berry 1992), or latent hostility toward the adoptee (Schneider and Rimmer 1984). DeGiulio, for example, emphasizes that "acceptance of self has been closely linked to acceptance of others," but she does not consider the importance of acceptance *by* others—that is, the effect of stigmatizing attitudes on the adoptive parents' self-acceptance. Even researchers who have recognized issues concerning disclosure of the adoption outside the family and the adoptee's awareness of the social meaning of adoption (Hajal and Rosenberg 1991; LeVine and Sallee 1990) have not noted the full extent to which adoptive parents are subject to stigmatizing attitudes and contradictory agency practices (see Kirk 1964). In a recent review of longitudinal adoption research (Berry 1992), environmental (i.e., cultural) variables are virtually absent.

As has been noted, adoption experts have referred to antisocial behaviors and undesirable personality traits in adoptees as the adopted child syndrome. According to David Kirschner, the adoptee's inability to integrate two parental images (often a "bad" set and a "good" set) is amplified by the adoptive parents' tendency to project their own unacceptable impulses onto the adoptee and the birth parents and by the general "family tendency towards repression and denial" (Kirschner 1992, 326; see also Kirschner and Nagel 1988). Consequently, Kirschner argues, adoptees run a greater risk than nonadopted persons of possessing such negative personality characteristics as pathological lying, manipulativeness, shallowness of attachment, a lack of meaningful relationships, stealing, truancy, promiscuity, academic underachievement or learning problems, pyromania, provocative behavior toward parents, teachers, and other authority figures, and generally antisocial behavior (Kirschner and Nagel 1988, 302–03).

Yet, the notion of the adopted child syndrome has been the focus of some debate. The National Committee for Adoption (1989) goes so far as to maintain that no such syndrome exists. Some of Kirschner's case studies (esp. 1992) include only adoptees with severe symptoms of psychopathology, and his findings therefore do not characterize adoptees in general. Still, they tend to stigmatize all adoptees (NCFA 1989, 206). By his definition, all adoptees are potentially at risk for the adopted child syndrome simply because they are adopted. Important social factors such as cultural images and attitudes tend to remain hidden; if included, they have generally been considered secondary or derivative pathogenic sources. He also fails to account for agency practices that may affect the adoptee. Many of these studies reinforce cultural stereotypes of women as mothers. First, they reflect an underlying concept that a woman's primary role is that of childbearer. Most of the studies assume that it is the adoptive mother who is infertile; little if any attention is given to the possible infertility of the adoptive father or, for that matter, to other possible reasons for adoption. Second, the dilemmas of adoption are interpreted as the results of the psychopathology of individual parents rather than as social reactions to infertility, as manifestations of or ways of coping with a social stigma (Greil, Leitko, and Porter 1988; Miall 1987). Adoption researchers, and presumably adoption case workers, have tended to forget that the adopters' problems stem not solely from their *individual* failure to accept infertility but also from a sense, rooted in the social values of the society in which they live, that they are not entitled to their children. Rather, adoption research has mirrored the enduring assumption that women's behavior and mental health are determined by their reproductive capacities (see Ussher 1990, 99).

APPLICATIONS OF *SHARED FATE*

The first studies of adoption and mental health, as has been noted, were based on the normative assumption that an adoptive mother's failure to adjust to infertility was the main cause, or at least a major cause, of psychological disturbances among adopted children. And even though one no longer hears references to the "narcissistic mortification" of "infertile women," the mother's psychological adjustment to infertility continues to be regarded as the decisive variable in determining or explaining the success or failure of an adoption (Miall 1986; Daly 1990).

In recent adoption research, the most revealing example of adoption experts' neglect of the significance of cultural attitudes and institutional arrangements in generating dilemmas of adoption is the response to the most widely cited sociological contribution to the field. In *Shared Fate* (1964), H. David Kirk noted that the adoptive parents he studied had developed "dichotomous patterns of defining adoption in response to the community's view of them and their children as different." He called these patterns "rejection of difference" and "acknowledgement of difference" and regarded them as ways of coping with the cultural disadvantages of adoptive parenthood. Kirk formulated a viewpoint that has since become central to the practice of adoption and a basic tenet of the adoption reform movement: that acknowledgment of the differences between adoptive and biological parenthood is more conducive to the adoptee's well-being than is denial of these differences. What has been disregarded in most of the subsequent adoption literature, however, is the source of the ambivalence, which Kirk located in the social context of adoption.

Within both the social work community and the community at large Kirk observed attitudes that required adopters to reject and acknowledge simultaneously the special aspects of adoptive parenthood. For example, although the social nature of parent-child bonding was stressed, the emphasis on the child's hereditary potential gave the adoptive parents mixed messages (Kirk 1964, 23). The chief contribution of Kirk's theory was to recognize the social character of the adoptive parents' coping strategies.

Not all social influences have been excluded from explanations of psychiatric disturbances among adoptees. Many researchers have indeed recognized that the scrutiny to which adoptive parents are subjected as part of the adoption process adds to the stress of the experience. However, no study has explored contradictory agency assumptions concerning the importance of the adoptee's heredity. And, with few exceptions, references to Kirk's work emphasize only one side of his argument: that the psychological well-being of adoptees is better served by the acknowledgment of difference (Dukette 1984; McRoy, Grotevant, and Zurcher 1988; Stein and Hoopes 1985).[10]

By neglecting the impact of the social stigmatization of adoption, some researchers have contributed to a pathologizing view of adoption. By failing to account for the impact of social and cultural norms and assumptions regarding infertility, childlessness, femininity, kinship, and the significance of the blood relation, some studies both reflect and reinforce a family ideology that defines adoptive bonds as inherently inferior to biological kinship. Paradoxically, researchers have perpetuated an image of the "normal family" to which adoptive families cannot measure up.

In addition to this entrenched view, however, two new developments can be observed in recent research on adoption and mental health. First, some adoption researchers have begun to stress the importance of developing multidimensional approaches to adoption and mental health, such as David Brodzinsky's (1990, 1993) stress and coping model. And second,

10. Whereas social and cultural influences are typically mentioned in the context of transracial adoptions, the social context of the difference of same-race adoptions is rarely noted.

there has also been increased emphasis on heredity in examining the emotional problems of adoptees, both in research (Cadoret 1990; Mednick, Gabrielli, and Hutchings 1984; Stewart 1990) and in the policy literature (McKelvey and Stevens 1994). Although it is not yet clear to what extent the renewed focus on genetic factors will dominate future discussions of adoption and mental health, the history of psychiatry shows that genetic explanations have tended to gain strong institutional support and have often outweighed other models.

The New Psychology of Adoption: The Search

In her 1976 survey of adoption agency policies and opinions, Mary Ann Jones reported that the principle of confidentiality was still widely supported. Over half of the agencies believed that the biological mothers' right to anonymity outweighed the adoptees' right to search; only 27 percent of the agencies believed that adult adoptees' rights were paramount (22). At the time, however, many agencies also believed that a change toward greater openness was inevitable. Although the sealed records debate has not been settled and although adoptees' birth records remain sealed in all but three states, the social work community has taken an increasingly sympathetic stance toward adoptees' need to search, to such an extent that the search is no longer considered a sign of pathology in the clinical literature. Some adoption case workers also question the contention that previous promises of confidentiality are morally binding. As Ken Watson, a former supporter of sealed records, argued in his keynote address to the 1992 conference of the North American Council on Adoptable Children, "If I had sold asbestos 25 or 30 years ago in good faith, I not only [would] have an obligation to stop selling asbestos now, I think I [would] have an obligation to go back to people I sold asbestos to and say, 'You know what? I was wrong. I did something that could harm you. Let's try to set it right.' "

As early as the mid-1970s, some adoption and mental health experts, in particular the research team of Arthur Sorosky, Annette Baran, and Reuben Pannor (1975), had published articles in professional journals in support of the searchers. They argued that searching fills an important function for resolving identity conflicts in adoptees and that the need to search is natural, not pathological. This position contrasted starkly with earlier studies, which had assumed that the need to search was a symptom of underlying mental health problems (such as an unresolved oedipal conflict).[11] Pannor, Baran, and Sorosky (1978) also questioned the common assumption that birth parents desire anonymity and noted that few studies have shown this to be true.

In 1978, the Child Welfare League of America stated for the first time that "adopted children are entitled to information about their birth, their birth family, significant genetic and social history, their placements, and the circumstances of their adoption" (Cole and Donley 1990, 281). Adoption experts were far from unanimous, however, in their support of openness,[12] and some have continued to express opposition (Byrd 1988) or at least caution regarding the new trend toward disclosure. Although there is little agreement about search procedures— for example, whether mutual-consent registries are sufficient and whether adoption agencies should be involved in the search process—the overwhelmingly positive outcome of reunions between adoptees and one or both birth parents (usually the birth

11. For a detailed overview of the literature on searching, see Schechter and Bertocci (1990).

12. As the various viewpoints expressed in a special 1979 issue of *Public Welfare* indicate.

mother) reported by researchers have led many adoption agencies, as well as some courts, to reevaluate the legitimacy of the sealed records policy. As stated earlier, however, regardless of such encouraging reports, the most recent attempt by the National Conference of Commissioners on Uniform State Laws to create a Uniform Adoption Act stipulates that adoption records remain sealed (National Conference of Commissioners on Uniform State Laws 1994, 146).

The actual number of searchers is, as noted, impossible to estimate, and some search activists and experts confidently claim that "most adoptees, either as children or adults, would like to meet their birth parents" (Auth and Zaret 1986, 567). Yet, studies in Great Britain, where birth certificates are available to adoptees upon request, have shown that although the number of searchers in any given year may be be as low as 1 percent, about 15 percent of all adoptees search sometime during their lifetime. Studies in Canada and the United States have reported that 32–35 percent of adoptees wish to search (Schechter and Bertocci 1990, 67). Neither is it known how many birth parents are searching for children relinquished in adoption, although it is clear that mothers constitute the overwhelming majority. Although adoptees seem to constitute the majority of searchers, it is interesting to note that by 1986 three times more birth parents than adoptees had registered in the International Soundex Reunion Registry (Gonyo and Watson 1988, 17).

Adoptees who do search are predominantly white, middle-class females in young adulthood. Studies have also shown that searchers tend to be dissatisfied with the way their adoptive parents had communicated issues relating to adoption, although this feeling should not be interpreted as dissatisfaction with the adoptive family itself (Bertocci and Schechter 1991, 181). The overwhelming majority initiate the search for the biological mother (Sachdev 1992, 60). Most adoptees who delay the search do so out of fear of hurting the adoptive parents. Yet studies suggest that a completed search often improves the relationship with the adoptive parents (e.g., Campbell, Silverman, and Patti 1991) or at least does not harm it (Sachdev 1992, 64). Some researchers have argued that the desire to search follows from negative experiences of adoption (Triseliotis 1973), such as a traumatic adoption revelation, strained adoptive family relationships, poor self-concept, and stressful life events (Sobol and Cardiff 1983). At least one study of personality differences between searchers and nonsearchers found that nonsearchers had more positive self-concepts than the searchers and that nonsearching adult adoptees had more positive feelings about being adopted and about their adoptive parents (Aumend and Barrett 1984).

Yet research has also indicated that the desire to search cannot be attributed solely, or primarily, to negative experiences of adoption. In some cases, it might simply be a matter of curiosity. Search activists argue, however, that the search expresses a natural and basic human need to experience connectedness, "to know one's own story" (Andersen 1988), and to fill an existential void (Kowal and Shilling 1985). In their writings in support of the search, Sorosky, Baran, and Pannor (e.g., 1975) have emphasized that although the decision to search might be linked to identity problems, this desire should be interpreted not as a pathological symptom but as an inevitable result of separation from the biological parents. Miriam Reitz and Kenneth Watson (1992, 237) summarize the main motives behind adoptees' need to search as "(1) the need to know why they were abandoned to adoption; (2) the unique genetic tie to the birth mothers and their need for continuity with their own history; and (3) the need to bring together the disparate pieces of their backgrounds in order to feel that they are whole and worthwhile beings."

The desire to search also tends to be triggered by life events such as pregnancy (Campbell, Silverman, and Patti 1991), which helps account for the greater number of female searchers. Exposure to activist groups is itself a powerful factor that promotes curiosity about the birth parents (Sachdev 1989, 84). Building on Carol Gilligan's (1982) argument concerning gender differences in moral reasoning, it is possible that women's gender-specific experiences have influenced their moral reasoning and that they therefore are less likely to view the decision to give up a child for adoption as a definite contractual agreement (a stance that seems more common among male adoptees; Wegar 1992, 99). Most research on searching and mental health, however, has not taken such contextual factors into account but has perceived adoptees' desires as expressions of innate needs.

The great success of reunions between adoptees and their birth parents is reflected in both the searchers' well-being and the subsequent quality of family relationships (Campbell, Silverman, and Patti 1991; Pacheco and Eme 1993). Even though some adoptees have expressed disillusionment to the extent that they felt unable to identify with the biological mother, reunions are still generally perceived as satisfying. But meeting one's biological mother does not guarantee that the adoptee will establish a close relationship with her. In his study of 124 Canadian searchers, Paul Sachdev (1989, 63) reported that half of these reunited relatives continued to see one another regularly, that 21 percent saw each other occasionally, and that 17 percent terminated the relationship after the first meeting. Nearly half described the relationship to the biological mother as a friendship; one-third regarded her as an acquaintance or a stranger; and one-fifth established a traditional mother-child relationship. It should also be noted that most of those in the last group were not close to their adoptive mothers. Although these findings cannot be generalized, it is clear that both reunion experiences and subsequent relationships vary considerably.

Most studies and public accounts of searching have been based on the experiences of individuals who have already expressed an interest in searching—that is, self-selected. We therefore know little about the experiences of those who do not search. Search activists generally have stressed that the need to know or meet one's biological parents is innate and that secrecy is a form of emotional abuse, but there are adoptees and birth parents who do not find this argument compelling. As one adoptee said, "I don't care to find my birthparents. I am not bitter toward them—they did the right thing for me. But who cares who they are? It doesn't matter where you got your hair color from. What matters is who loved you and took care of you" (Hicks 1995).

Because most adoption research to date has focused either on adoptees with mental health problems or on searchers, our understanding of experiences of adoption and the search remains partial. Also, it is important to stress that an adoptee's wish to know his or her biological parents does not necessarily mean that he or she fully accepts the search activists' arguments. Adoptees of course have a variety of needs, and the need to know is not necessarily the same as the need to search. In the search movement literature, however, the need to search is generally presented as universal.

As I noted in chapter 1, both the clinical and the activist literature on searching typically depicts searchers and nonsearchers as fundamentally different groups with regard to psychological disposition[13] or experiences of adoption. The

13. Lifton (1988, 75), for example, has argued that nonsearchers, by their very nature, are less inquisitive, more passive and self-denigrating (as they accept "society's mandate that they should not know something as primal as who gave birth to them"), and more oppressed by internalized guilt than are searchers.

complex and ambivalent nature of adoptees' experiences has consequently often been misunderstood. Although it makes sense to distinguish between negative and positive opinions about searching, the tendency to dichotomize hides the interplay of motives that influence the choice. Because researchers have been interested primarily in what motivates adoptees to seek information about or to meet their biological parents (assuming that one set of motives is so dominant that ambivalence regarding the search is irrelevant or does not exist), they have missed the complexity of adoptees' feelings and how they reflect society's definitions of family and kinship. As Judith Modell (1994) notes, many adoptees do not regard concepts such as "mother" and "father" as abstract but link them to specific behaviors. In contrast to search activists who define searchers as partly "motherless" (Lifton 1994, 13–20, 165), some adoptees who search want to reserve the concept of "mother" for their adoptive mothers, who have nurtured them. American family ideology so clearly distinguishes between biological and social bonds, however, that it would not be surprising if adoptees tended to experience the ambivalence provoked by these concepts as problematic rather than broadening. As anthropologists know, the existence of several "mothers" and "fathers" constitutes less of a strain in societies where adoption is a major means of forming kinship bonds. On the other hand, ambivalence is central to experiences of adoption in societies where family is equated with biological kin and kinship is defined by the blood tie (Wegar 1992, 96).

EXPERTS AND ACTIVISTS: AN UNEASY ALLIANCE

Although search activists have been critical of adoption research and practices that have legitimated the sealing of adoption records, they have also depended upon this tradition of research to legitimate their own claims.[14] Since the 1960s, experts have been used increasingly in court battles over the existence of "good cause" (see chap. 2; Mason 1994, 175); this trend has also shaped the search debate. The most important argument presented in favor of the disclosure of identifying information has been that genealogical knowledge is necessary for the development of normal identity (Sachdev 1989, 10). This argument has two components. First, since most adoptees do not know their biological relatives, adoptees as a group are portrayed as severely psychologically afflicted. Against this background we can understand statements such as the one made by the president of the American Adoption Congress: "Adoptees as a group have a higher anxiety level than prisoners of war" (*Donahue* 1991, 7). Second, the causes of psychological afflictions are attributed to the adoption per se, whereas the dilemmas and contradictions perpetuated by the social context are not explored.[15] Both arguments lend credibility to the argument that the sealed records policy is faulty, and both have been bol-

14. As sociological studies of claims-making processes have shown, expert opinions play a central role in the legitimation of social problems; see, for example, Johnson (1989).

15. The importance of genealogical information has frequently been compared to the struggles of various ethnic groups to rediscover and assert their "roots" (e.g., Sachdev 1989, 13). Yet, there is a major difference between arguments supporting struggles to discover ethnic identities and the claims presented in favor of adoptees' rights to have access to genealogical information. In the struggle to reclaim ethnic roots, activists have argued that the negative or limiting aspects of their current identity have been imposed by attitudes and stereotypes held by the dominant culture. In the struggle over adoption reform, however, explanations of adoptees' identity struggles have seldom reached beyond the adoptive family and fail to include the impact of cultural images and conflicting demands that shape the experiences of adoptees, birth parents, and adoptive parents.

stered by references to the clinical literature. By emphasizing the psychopathology of adoption in their research, experts who took the sealed records policy for granted nevertheless laid the theoretical groundwork for the search activists' critique of the adoption system.

Despite the increasing interest in the search among social workers and mental health professionals, and the at least partial normalization of the search in the clinical literature, the relationship between adoption agencies and search activists remains strained. Developments in the adoption field have seldom emerged solely as responses to adoptees' best interests; rather, they have tended to be the result of multiple external factors such as the increase in the number of childless couples wanting to adopt and social workers' pursuit of professional status. Also the current interest in issues of searching reflects a concern with the professional future of social work, especially in light of the growing number of independent adoptions.

In 1951, 53 percent of all unrelated adoptions were independently arranged (by doctors, lawyers, or clergy), 29 percent were handled by private adoption agencies, and only 18 percent were arranged by public agencies. By 1972, the number of such adoptions handled by public agencies had doubled, and since then it has remained relatively stable, at just under 40 percent (Stolley 1993, 30). Currently, independent placements account for two-thirds of newborn adoptions, and public adoption agencies are primarily involved in the placement of children with special needs (Schulman and Behrman 1993, 14). During the 1980s, the number of independent adoptions increased more than agency adoptions. These trends have caused considerable concern among adoption professionals.

Although the reasons behind the increasing number of independent adoptions have not been studied, it seems likely that the change was prompted by changing community attitudes toward unwed mothers, a general shift toward openness in adoption, and the growing discrepancy between the number of prospective adopters and the number of adoptable infants. Although proponents of independent adoptions have argued that they foster greater equality and openness in the adoption system, agency advocates have consistently maintained that independently arranged adoptions involve greater risks for all parties involved, primarily because of the lack of professional counseling before and after the adoption. Jean Emery (1993), a former director of the adoption program of the Child Welfare League of America, argued that "unlike agency adoption, independent adoption agents most often view adults as the primary clients and tend to see their job as simply finding babies for couples. . . . Independent agents who process adoptions are also less likely than trained and experienced social workers to understand the seriousness of the adoption process." Clearly, the escalating number of nonagency adoptions and public criticism of the sealed records policy constitute major threats to the social work profession. Social work's new interest in and even advocacy of the search reflect not only a sincere concern with adoptees' well-being but also a will to retain adoption as a professional specialty through the development of new methods to facilitate the search process. Some mental health professionals have argued that any type of compulsory intermediary system, such as testing of the adoptees' motives for undertaking a search, abrogates the adoptees' right to self-determination (Schechter and Bertocci 1990, 88), but many have suggested that social workers should develop the expertise necessary to take on their new role as search experts (e.g., Sachdev 1989, 196). To some extent this change benefits the searchers, but the situation in other countries reveals that this development is not always beneficial. In Great Britain, adoptees gained the right to see identifying information in 1975, but only after they agreed to counseling from clinically trained social workers. As Erica Haimes and Noel Timms (1985, 80–81) argue, this very process implies that adoptees are potentially damaged individuals and furthermore attributes any emotional problems or conflicts to the adoptees themselves. Although counseling might benefit some adoptees, laws and practices that mandate counseling and presume the existence of emotional pathology continue to stigmatize adoption and adoptees.

4

Debating Sealed Records

THE SOCIAL CONSTRUCTION OF

SEARCH NARRATIVES

In the past twenty years the sealed records issue has become part of the public discourse on social problems. Whereas the collection of adoptees' life histories compiled by Jean Paton in the 1950s roused little serious interest among social workers or in the media, today adoption stories are dramatically recounted throughout the media. The adoption theme, particularly the theme of searching for birth parents, has emerged as a compelling human-interest story and has inspired myriad novels, plays, and movies. This publicity is essential to the search movement: not only does it evoke sympathy and support, but it promotes curiosity among adoptees about their biological origins (Sachdev 1989, 84).

The search movement has not yet reached its goal of overturning sealed records laws, but search activists have been extraordinarily successful in attracting attention to their claims by tapping into American ideals and values. The lack of interest and understanding, and the sometimes utter dismissal, that characterized earlier lay and professional attitudes toward adoptees' need to search have increasingly been replaced by supportive postures. In the clinical and popular literature, the desire to search is no longer perceived as unreasonable or as symptomatic of underlying pathology; today a *lack* of interest in one's biological origins or offspring is often perceived as a sign of repression.

Since the late 1960s minority groups in the United States have insisted on the importance of ethnic roots as a source of identity. This movement has also promoted sympathy for adoptees in their search for biological kin (Feigelman and Silverman 1983, 196). Public sympathy cannot, however, be explained solely by Americans' interest in the search for ethnic roots. The debate over adoption reform serves as a symbolic battleground for conflicting perceptions of the nature of kinship, identity, and attachment. In this chapter I explore the rhetorical strategies employed in the adoption debate, focusing in particular on the construction of a public identity for the search movement through self-narratives. As the literature on the new social movements suggests, "identities do not pre-exist movements so much as take shape with them" (Gamson 1995, 296). In their critique of the adoption system, search activists define and redefine for themselves and for the American public what it means to be adopted.

The analysis of the clinical literature on adoption in chapter 3 showed that scientific theories about adoption and mental health mirror society's view that real kinship is biologically based. This kind of cultural resonance is particularly important for social movements. And, as we saw in the introduction, the construction of a collective identity is especially central to new social movements, which, like the search movement, empower members to "name themselves" and "reclaim a self robbed of its identity" (Johnston, Laraña, and Gusfield 1994, 10). Also, identities and motives are shaped by the culture's narrative resources and widely held beliefs. When social-movement activists construct their arguments and their collective identity, they draw upon and elaborate on existing cultural scripts. Such collective public identities are a complex mix of new and old elements. This chapter shows that the search movement has replaced the negative cultural images of adoptees as "bad seeds" by positive images of adoptees as survivors and mythic heroes (Lifton 1988, 39, 29). The way search activists construct such positive images, however, does not erase existing definitions of adoption as an inferior means of family formation but, rather, utilizes them.

THE POLITICS OF LIFE STORIES

The political significance of autobiographies or self-narratives can be seen in the case of many modern social movements (see Olney 1980, 13). For members of marginalized social groups, the recounting of personal life experiences is often the only means of making their voices heard or of formulating experiences independently of dominant cultural and institutional frameworks.[1] By offering privileged access to experiences that cannot be articulated through existing channels of political expression, life stories constitute an alternative route and incentive to political change.

Autobiographical accounts have been instrumental in the mobilization of the search movement, and their human-interest potential and cultural resonance have attracted publicity in the media. By revealing the personal quandaries of adoptees who have been denied the opportunity to search for their biological origins, search activists have presented a picture of American adoption that stands in stark contrast to the positive image traditionally presented by adoption agencies and child welfare organizations. They have also described for the first time the

1. Yet, as the feminist sociologist Dorothy Smith (1987) has forcefully argued, sociologists have contributed to the marginal position of women by failing to take seriously women's experiences as a basis for inquiry. Others have observed that the methodological rituals of social scientific research in general suppress respondents' stories and in this way reinforce the marginalization of oppressed social groups (Mishler 1986).

institution of adoption from the viewpoint of the adopted. As Jean Paton (1954) phrased the argument,

> Everyone except the adopted has been talking about adoption. About certain parts of adoption, the parts that can be seen and the parts that can be heard. The rest is silence—or was.
>
> What other human institution has so little comment from those within it? Of what other group is so much said from without and so little from within? How has it been that the adopted seem to have had nothing to say, whereas it is conspicuous herein that they have waited only for an invitation, and that their thoughts have been long?

In the early 1970s, the effort to reform sealed records laws and agency practices was spurred by two influential autobiographical accounts of the psychological effects of the sealed records policy, Florence Fisher's *The Search for Anna Fisher* (1973) and Betty Jean Lifton's *Twice Born: Memoirs of an Adopted Daughter* (1977). More recent examples are *An Adopted Woman,* by Katrina Maxtone-Graham (1983) and *Letters to My Birthmother* (1991), by Amy Dean. Birth mothers in search of their adopted children have also contributed autobiographical accounts, of which Lorraine Dusky's *Birthmark* (1979) is probably the best known and Carol Schaefer's *The Other Mother: A True Story* (1992) is the most recent.

Well before the social work profession reevaluated its views regarding open records and searching, the search issue began to be featured frequently in newspapers, in popular magazines such as *Newsweek, Time,* and *Reader's Digest,* and in various other periodicals devoted to women's issues and health. The human-interest aspect of the search narratives of adoptees and birth parents has attracted the attention of all the major news magazines: "For adoptee Donna Cullom, the search for the woman who had borne her three decades earlier lasted twelve long years" (Francke 1975); "Susan Long, known as Baby Girl Foster when she was born, is an adoptee who recently went on a search for her lost past" (Lifton 1976); "Patricia Szymczak was 36 years old when she decided to pursue a quest she had contemplated since childhood: finding her mother" (Taylor 1989).

Search narratives have been essential in exposing injustices in the adoption system. They have produced new insights about adoption, without which adoption agencies and legislators would not have reconsidered their stance on confidentiality. Meetings of adoption search groups are based on storytelling (Modell 1992), and activist newsletters are editorially organized around so-called found stories, the most common type of search narrative (see, e.g., ALMA 1990). Exemplary life stories have provided searchers with motivation and "the means by which identities may be fashioned" (Rosenwald and Ochberg 1992, 1). By phrasing their struggles in terms of the ethos of individual freedom, choice, and self-fulfillment, activists have reintroduced the issue of searching in a culturally acceptable form. Yet, by reinforcing the dominant cultural characterization of adoption as an inferior family form, search narratives have so far tended to reinforce the social stigmatization of adoption. As Elizabeth Bartholet (1993) has observed, the search movement has created "new sources of stigma" for adoption.

To some extent, this stigma may have been imposed or bolstered by how the media has framed and interpreted the search issue. The mere act of bringing issues into the realm of public discourse is problematic, because experts (Foucault 1978) and the mass media (Gitlin 1979) tend to interpret or reinscribe experiences in terms of dominant norms and explanations. For example, in spite of their emancipatory potential, the stories and experiences of rape survivors have often been channeled into public discourse in ways that have reinforced widely held beliefs about women as accomplices to rape and incest (Alcoff and Grey 1993). Life stories can serve as forms of empowerment while at the same time re-creating dominant structures, but self-help groups and social movements can also wittingly or unwittingly reinforce dominant interpretations. Consider the problem of addiction: by framing such problems in individual terms, co-dependency self-help groups have overlooked the societal problems that contribute to addiction and have thus inadvertently blamed the victims (Rice 1992). My analysis of representations of adoption and the search in popular culture (chap. 5) shows that search narratives have also been framed in such a way as to dramatize and highlight individual characteristics while leaving the underlying systemic causes untouched.

Because of the reactionary thrust of political rhetoric, activists and reformers also risk reinforcing confining labels of difference that others before them have used.[2] On the other hand,

2. In his study of the rhetoric of social movements, Cathcart (1980) argued that many collective activities labeled as reform movements are not reform movements at all, because their rhetoric is primarily aimed at adjusting the existing order rather than rejecting it. He distinguishes between two forms of reformist rhetoric, managerial and confrontational. According to Cathcart, it is the latter type of rhetoric that distinguishes the true reform movement. Movements utilizing the vocabulary of managerial rhetoric, on the other hand, are characterized by the "keeping of the secret," a notion he borrows from Kenneth Burke. In contrast to confrontational rhetoric, managerial rhetoric "accepts that the order has a code of control which must not be destroyed, while at the same time striving to gain acceptance of that which will perfect (or restore to perfection) the system" (441). In fact, *not* to challenge taken-for-granted cognitive cultural frameworks might be essential to the success of a movement. Theorists of persuasion believe that audiences are first and foremost persuaded by appeals to preexisting "cognitive schemata," that is, pre-

vocabularies of liberation reveal that the activist, far from being "the author of the ideology or discourse which she is speaking" (Weedon 1987, 31), by necessity draws upon and reproduces prior and independently existing meanings.

In their efforts to change the sealed records policy, search activists have appropriated widely shared symbols, metaphors, and core social values. Like other public debates, the debate over adoption reform is "waged with metaphors, catch phrases, and other symbolic devices that mutually support an interpretive package for making sense of an ongoing stream of events as they relate to a particular issue" (see Gamson and Stuart 1992, 59). As Hilgartner and Bosk (1988, 64) have noted, "Some problems may be easier to relate to deep mythic themes, and they thus provide better material to ponder collectively."[3]

To Search or Not to Search: Moral Vocabularies of Motive

Life stories do not simply reflect their author's experiences; they are also part of the construction of these experiences and the author's identity. As George C. Rosenwald (1992) noted, "When people tell life stories, they do so in accordance with models of intelligibility specific to the culture. Without such

---

vious beliefs and values that are latent (or not so latent): "Even when challenging existing attitudes and values, a rhetorical effort must rely on some of those values and attitudes" (Condit 1990, 25; see also Smith 1982, 27–53). This paradox of emancipatory rhetoric reveals a tension between modern and postmodern aspects of social movements. On the one hand, the emergence and endurance of social movements certifies that "[in] the narrative of self-discovery . . . issues of autonomy and self-emancipation possess a continuing and often urgent relevance for marginalized social groups" (Felski 1989, 237).

3. Such "frame alignment" strategies are also essential to recruiting new members or participants to the movement (Snow et al. 1986).

models narration is impossible. These models are consonant with the forces that stabilize the given organization of society. Stories that comply with such cultural models are generally recognized as sensible. Their formal compliance with these models go unnoticed: they simply make sense. By contrast, stories that fail to conform to the models are more or less alarming" (265).

But although autobiographics represent the author's effort to give meaning to his or her "mythic tale" (Gusdorf 1980, 48), the rhetorical nature of personal narratives should not be interpreted as a sign of lacking sincerity or authenticity. Rhetoric is an integral and necessary part of human communication (see Fish 1989, 471–502). What we can and must do, however, is to analyze critically the connections between particular styles of self-representation, on the one hand, and beliefs, values and power relations in society, on the other.

Like many other contemporary social movements, the search movement emerged "in defense of identity" (Johnston, Laraña, and Gusfield 1994, 10), and identity concerns are indeed central to the agenda and rhetoric of the movement. In this section I explore how search activists publicly define what it means to be adopted and what motivates them to search. I draw upon two related traditions of sociological inquiry: the poststructuralist critique of methodological realism and the constructionist analysis of autobiographies. The first assumes that knowledge of authentic inner motives is not possible except as mediated by "the discourses that we speak/speak us" (Silverman 1989, 38).[4] As sociologists, therefore, our task is not to explain nar-

4. As early as 1940, Mills observed that rather than "interpreting actions and language as external manifestations of subjective and deeper lying elements in individuals, the [sociologist's] research task is the locating of particular types of action within typal frames of normative actions and socially situated clusters of motive" (913). Mills relied on Kenneth Burke's definition of motives, not as sources of behavior but

ratives about motives in terms of the authors' hidden mental states but "to determine why it was meaningful for some things to be said and for others not to be said" in a given social context (Wuthnow 1987, 63). Like other narratives, adoptees' life and search stories are framed by widely shared cultural vocabularies and conventions: "Through such narratives people are brought to the point of wanting what they must want in their society as well as to regard these wants as reasonable" (Rosenwald 1992, 265).

In the sealed records debate, arguments in favor of and against the importance of searching (and the legitimacy of the sealed records policy) often express two different and opposing moral vocabularies: the ethic of reciprocity and the ethic of self-discovery (Wegar 1992). Or, to use comparable notions developed by Robert Wuthnow (1987, 201), the ethic of individualism and the ethic of individuality. In Wuthnow's definition, "individualism emphasizes a concern for the moral responsibility of individuals toward other individuals, whereas individuality focuses on the moral responsibility of the individual toward his or her own self."

The ethic of reciprocity is, of course, not peculiar to adoptive kinship but is an integral part of human relationships in general. In the case of adoption, however, this particular moral vocabulary, or at least the force of the vocabulary, can be traced to the social function of adoption in the United States. In contrast to adoption practices in other cultures, the institutionalization of adoption in the United States in the nineteenth century was legitimized primarily by references to the best interests of the child (see chap. 2). By implicitly indicating a debt of gratitude, the child-rescue aspect of adoption has probably made it

---

rather as "concept[s] used by people to make actions understandable to them and to others" (Gusfield 1989, 11).

less socially acceptable for adoptees to pursue their genealogical interests independently of their adoptive parents' wishes. In one court dispute over the disclosure of adoption records, the judge argued that the "adoptive parents need and deserve the child's loyalty as they grow older" (Tartanella 1982, 473). The image of adoptees as having been rescued by their parents has most likely reinforced the legitimacy of the ethic of reciprocity.

In contrast, search activists have framed their life stories in terms of the ethic of self-discovery, which is central to many other right-to-access movements as well. The moral vocabulary employed by adoption reform activists carries an emancipatory political force. To argue in terms of the ethic of self-discovery constitutes an attempt to reframe the issue of secrecy in adoption and to account for the neglected and stifled interests of adoptees.[5] The emancipatory discourse of self-discovery reflects a broader cultural preoccupation with the search for identity or the individual's moral right to embark upon this quest. Ideological or not, the pursuit of "finding oneself" has become a moral phenomenon in modern social life, as the morality of self-actualization both shapes and is shaped by the "institutions of modernity" (Giddens 1991, 79). One reason that search narratives in today's public and expert discourse appear to be increasingly intelligible is that the moral vocabulary drawn upon by search activists—that is, the ethic of self-discovery—has become not only acceptable but perhaps even normative to the way Americans perceive the quest for identity.[6] By phrasing their arguments in terms of the ethic of self-discovery, search

5. At the same time, this emancipatory rhetoric has tended to distort the nature of adoptees' ambivalence by arguing that the ethic of self-discovery contains a more genuine expression of human nature than does the ethic of reciprocity.

6. The construction of life stories in Western society is also tied to "the form of human activity known as adventure" (Scheibe 1986, 130).

activists have emphasized the link between their specific arguments and the concerns of the general public. As Betty Jean Lifton argued in *Twice Born*, "Even blood children must one day go off on their own lonely journeys of self-discovery" (5).

Reframing the Search: From Confidentiality to Secrecy

Struggles over political power and social influence are often waged as struggles over symbols, metaphors, and the appropriation and interpretation of core social values. Rather than draw upon competing symbols to advance their arguments, opponents often propose different interpretations of the same symbols and ideographs. Studies of the political culture in the United States, for example, have shown that although Americans differ in party affiliation, there exists within the political culture a core of dominant symbolic configurations that serve as focal points for political debates (see McLeod 1990). By applying the language of cherished democratic principles, activists may both reveal idiosyncrasies in their opponents' arguments and redefine their own public image as servants of the public interest (Snow et al. 1986, 469).

In the debate over sealed records, both the search advocates and their opponents have argued that their views genuinely express the American ethos of individualism. Adoption professionals and policymakers who oppose change have argued that the desire of some adoptees to find their biological parents jeopardizes the social institution of adoption, which, according to their views, currently benefits the society as a whole. The sealed records policy has also been portrayed as an expression of the fluid American social structure and the right to re-create oneself. As Austin Foster (1979, 36) noted in arguing against the disclosure of identifying information: "One does not discover one's identity from history. Quite literally, we create our identity."[7] According to this point of view, the sealed records policy allows the adoptee to create his or her fate unfettered by origins—an opportunity that any true American should cherish.

In contrast, by positing the "social fiction" of adoption against the "natural desire" to search, activists have portrayed the adoptees' search for their biological origins as the triumph of the individual will to self-realization over the oppression of social arrangements. Sealed records laws and practices impinge not only upon adoptees' legal right to individual freedom and their "natural right" to genealogical knowledge but also upon the individual's right to self-discovery and self-realization. This argument, like the ethic of self-discovery, derives some of its rhetorical force from the single most basic story of Western civilization, the classical "monomyth," which describes a hero's struggle against obstacles and enemies (Gergen and Gergen 1983, 257). Moreover, the sealed records policy subverts the American model of democracy. As Florence Fisher (1973, 229) asked: "Where else in our free society is such secrecy condoned?"

Search activists have also appealed to the constitutional principle that persons cannot be treated as property. The doctrine of parens patriae, as well as the whole concept of child welfare, was introduced by American legislators in the late nineteenth century as a counterweight to the earlier notion of parents'

7. "Crises in identity are a recurring aspect of American life. . . . This is pandemic in our culture; it is not exclusively a problem of adopted children. However, an adopted child can easily convert the identity question, 'Who am I?' into the questions: 'Where did I come from?' 'Who are my ancestors?' 'What are my roots?' . . . Unfortunately this is a fallacious search because the identity crisis is an existential one. One does not discover one's identity from history. Quite literally, we create our identity."

(especially fathers') property rights in the child (Mason 1994). However, according to "The Eight Great Fallacies of Adoption," a pamphlet distributed by the ALMA Society (n.d.), the sealed records policy violates adoptees' right not to be treated as property by assuming that "an adoptee belongs to his or her new family forever . . . but belonging is a term used for property."

At least two other basic symbolic configurations[8] have shaped the adoption reformers' claims: the morality of truth and authenticity and the inviolability of the blood relation (see chap. 5). The quest for truth structures most search narratives: "I didn't look only for my mother and my father," writes Fisher (1973) in her autobiography; "I looked for the truth" (206): "Mother became less nervous as she talked. Truth is cleansing and her words began to flow freely" (217); "You're not rejecting me. You're rejecting . . . life and truth" (251); "More than other people, adoptees fear the consequences of venting their true feelings" (15). When founding ALMA in 1971, Fisher chose the slogan "The truth of his origins is the birthright of every man." On her decision to search, Lifton (1977, 5) writes, "I knew someday the awakened adult must prevail over the repressed child: that she would eventually take her place on the side of truth and history."

Since the first sealed records law was enacted, in 1917, the major argument for sealing adoption records has been that confidentiality benefits all the parties involved, including the state, as well as the public interest. Sealing the adoptees' birth certificates was intended to ensure the adoptive parents the "same rights to parental autonomy and family privacy that the birthparents once had" (Hollinger 1993, 49). By converting the issue of confidentiality into an issue of secrecy, a practice that was

8. For a discussion of this aspect of political rhetoric, see McLeod (1990).

formerly represented in positive terms became invested with negative social meanings. This transformation was made possible by linking claims for openness with the moral themes of sincerity, authenticity, and truthfulness.[9]

The Dramatic Structure of Search Narratives

There are considerable similarities in the ways people tell their life stories. Narratives are typically composed of events that are linked causally and lead to a valued end point (Gergen and Gergen 1983). In order to make a convincing case for the necessity of social reform, social activists also need a fund of evil and repulsive elements upon which to draw when they build their protest narratives. Phrased in terms of Kenneth Burke's classic formulation, a tension between "a good agent and an evil scene" is necessary to legitimate altering the scene (Condit 1990, 27).

In search narratives, the searching adoptee or birth parent obviously represents a good agent, and the adoption agencies and the legal system the evil scene. Fisher (1973, 107) describes her encounter with the legal establishment in her unsuccessful attempt to gain access to genealogical information: "The clerk who took the authorization note was quite small, about five-foot-two; he was a dapper little man with patent-leather hair, a small, neat, oiled moustache, and a tight suit jacket on his small frame. He reminded me of an otter or a weasel, or a gloating hotel clerk in a Grade B movie." As a personification of the legal establishment, the weaselly clerk is as an effective symbol for the social arrangement he is hired to protect. Often, but not always, the adoptive parents are also part of the evil scene. In "The Eight Great Fallacies of Adoption," it is argued

9. Trilling, for example, proposed "the idea that at a certain point in its history the moral life of Europe added to itself a new element, the state or quality of the self which we call sincerity" (1972, 2).

that "sealed records, whatever you may have heard about them, were actually designed to keep the adoptive parents happy— free from the worry that someone would take their hard-won children away from them." Or, as Lifton states the argument (1977, 13): "At first secrecy was rationalized as a means of hiding the shame of the child's illegitimacy, but in recent years it seems to have had more to do with the adoptive parents' emotional need to live *as if* they had produced offspring of their own."

Yet, of all the agents depicted in search narratives, the image of adoptive parents remains the most ambiguous: they are alternately portrayed as victims and villains. Unlike some critics of the sealed records policy, the search activist Hal Aigner (1986, 155) has argued that "perhaps the most striking aspect of the adoptive parents' place in the greater scheme of American adoption is that they have apparently been lacking in advocates." Yet he sets a negative tone for his chapter on adoptive parents by beginning with an account of abuse in adoptive families.

During the past decade the American public has been increasingly captivated by "the DNA mystique," to use the term coined by Dorothy Nelkin and Susan Lindee (1995). In American popular culture, biological or genetic explanations are currently granted unprecedented explanatory power, particularly in matters concerning the family and self-identity. As Nelkin and Lindee note, the adoption-search movement has effectively capitalized on the strong cultural currency of the gene, and genetic determinism has been central to the activists claims (58–78). In the search-movement literature, the biological need and the (in)ability to reproduce are also important conveyers of meaning. Although the adoptive parents' desire to have a child is seen as understandable and natural, their involuntary childlessness sets them apart from the order of nature. In order to distinguish the adoptive parents' illegitimate need to act "*as if* they had produced offspring of their own" from the legitimate need of adoptees and birth parents to reunite, they must be depicted as different. This difference has typically been attributed to the biological inability of the adoptive parents (in particular the adoptive mother) to conceive. This focus on natural or intrinsic difference rather than on the social norms that shape experiences of childlessness and adoption has led adoption reformers to disregard the extent to which adoption practices are circumscribed by cultural conventions and power relations in society at large. Not only search activists but also adoptive parents have in some respects benefited from the view of childlessness as an "unnatural" state. Despite references to the child's best interests, adoption professionals have traditionally regarded the prospective adopters' "natural" craving for a child as the most legitimate motive for adoption.

Search narratives also closely resemble the type of autobiography known as "conversion narrative." Lifton, for example, writes about her intensifying desire to search in terms of a "rebirth" (1977, 145), and Fisher speaks of the clues to her biological origins as "the light" (1973, 74). Since a central part of the search activists' argument has been that the desire for genealogical information is not only a fundamental legal right but also a basic human need, it is important to explain why the decision to search occurred when it did and not earlier.[10] In contrast to the social arrangements surrounding the institution of

10. According to Griffin (1990, 152), authors who have undergone experiences of religious or secular conversion must "create myths of self that account plausibly for the dramatic shifts in attitude and behavior that follow from an authentic conversion experience." This dilemma is resolved by depicting the desire for information as, though at times latent, still universal and ever present: "Adoptees, when they learn they are adopted or when they become adults, *all* share two questions: 'Should I look?' and 'How should I look?'" (Fisher 1973, 73, my emphasis).

adoption, the need to search ultimately finds its base in nature: "What is more natural than the desire to learn something of one's heritage" (Fisher 1973, 14). The conversion constitutes the triumph of human nature over social arrangements and emphasizes the primacy of biological bonds over the other sources of attachment.

The conversion, or the decision to search, is a sign of maturity, and the adoptee who does not undergo the conversion remains a child forever (Lifton 1988, 81). This explains why some adoptees do not search—they are, by definition, "eternal children," "artificial," and "Uncle Tom[s]." They lack what the searchers share with the nonadopted population: the fundamental human need to connect with their "own kind" (51). They are truly different: "Nonsearchers, for all their sense of righteousness and loyalty, have always seemed to me self-denigrating. . . . There is the implication that they don't have a right to rock their own boat, to open their own can of worms. They seem to accept that they don't have a right to their own heritage. We see such internalized guilt in them that even if their adoptive parents should sanction a search, it would be hard for them to follow through. It is as if they have a will not to know" (75).

Like rhetoric, the use of metaphors is an essential element of human communication. Metaphors are central to the symbolic construction of reality and to the reproduction of society.[11] A metaphor frequently drawn upon by adoption reformers is the Holocaust. Marsha Riben (1988, 13) reflects on her reasons for writing *Shedding Light on the Dark Side of Adoption*, a book dedicated to the memory of Lisa Steinberg: "In answer to the question, 'Why this Book?' I am reminded of the Holocaust

11. According to Lakoff and Johnson (1980), our conceptual system (in terms of thought, language, and action) is basically metaphorical in nature.

survivor whose job had been to remove the dead bodies from the ovens. Just when he felt that he could take it no longer and was about to take his own life, a woman entering the gas chamber said to him: 'You cannot die, for if there are no survivors there will be no one to testify.' With no one to testify, the death of six million might have been denied to have happened at all, and worse yet, repeated."

Using the same metaphor, Lifton (1988, 39) argues: "It could be said that all Adoptees are survivors of a holocaust of one kind or another." But holocausts cannot be of one kind or another. There is only one kind of Holocaust, and this is precisely what makes the metaphor.

BLOOD TIES: THE SACRED BOND

Effective arguments cannot explore subtle cases but must emphasize the strong examples based on widely shared assumptions (see Condit 1990, 26). The much-publicized beating death of Lisa Steinberg by her adoptive father in 1987 is an example of an event that drew attention to the problems of secrecy in adoption. Riben (1988, 41) argues that the Steinberg case should be seen not as an isolated incident but as reflective of a more general pattern of abuse within adoptive families, abuse that has been further perpetuated by the practice of sealing adoption records.

Riben defines adoption as the "absence of kinship" and hence clearly defines kinship in terms of the blood relation alone. The same notion has also been used by adoptees in describing their experiences of being adopted (see, e.g., ALMA 1988). Although Riben recognizes that "adoptive parents, as a group, should not be expected to be any better or worse than any other group of parents equally matched for age, financial resources, etc.," she goes on to argue, "If research were carried out carefully and correctly in this area we would be surprised to find that not only is child abuse just as prevalent among adopted as nonadopted parents but I would not be at all surprised to find that it is higher among adoptive parents. Firstly, because of the absence of kinship, and secondly, because of expectations" (1988, 40–41).

Riben bases her argument that the absence of biological bonds increases the risk of children being abused by their stepparents or adoptive parents on studies by behavioral biologists who have concluded that the lack of biological relationship explains the higher rate of infanticide among some animals by unrelated males (40).

In their attempts to overturn the sealed records policy, activists have drawn upon one of the basic tenets of American family ideology (Bernardes 1985): the inviolability of the biological bond. Lifton (1988, 81) writes that she has "seen Adoptees go through all these stages as if some law, as inexorable as the laws of physical science, were driving them home to the blood connection." In her most recent book, Lifton (1994, 8) observes that her research has led her to believe that "it is unnatural for members of the human species to grow up separated from and without knowledge of their natural clan."

Although Phyllis Chesler, in *Sacred Bond* (1989), explores primarily the issue of surrogacy, the chapter in which she compares surrogacy contracts and adoption contracts in terms of their legality epitomizes the search activists' argument. As the title of her book suggests, the search movement has justified its claims for opening the adoption files by referring to the inviolability of the blood relation—the sacred bond. The central question Chesler raises is whether any legal contract can overrule the biological bond between mother and child: "Are contracts sacred? And in particular: Are they more sacred than the bond between a mother and child?" (109).

Chesler's exclusive focus on the mother-child bond repre-

sents the broad trend of equating true parenthood with biological motherhood. As Judith Modell (1986, 228) observed,
"mother" has come to represent "parent" more generally in
American culture. Although the activist group Concerned
United Birthparents, among others, has made an effort to replace "mother" with "parent," the latter concept has not communicated the biological view of parent child bonding effectively (656). It should be noted that fathers (biological and
adoptive) are not absent from the search narratives, but the
close symbolic affinity among motherhood, the natural, and
blood ties makes the depiction of the mother-child, and particularly the mother-daughter, relationship especially significant. By so strongly emphasizing the genetic tie, however, this
equation reflects (at least in part) a patriarchal genetic definition of kinship that downplays the social character of parenting
(Rothman 1989, 39).

Lifton (1988, 81) argues that "the concept of motherhood is
difficult for female Adoptees. Even the word mother is loaded.
The woman who has never been born does not imagine giving
birth. The woman who has never known her biological mother
does not imagine becoming one. Her role model is the infertile mother. Her role is the eternal child." Reflecting on the
psychological problems of her own adoptive mother, she writes
in her autobiography: "Even now, years later, I who was that
frightened child, wonder if the intensity of that mother's hys-
teria was not the fruit of a barren womb" (1977, 15).

What is interesting in these quotes is not only the link among
biological motherhood, the natural, and the psychologically
healthy but Lifton's emphasis on her adoptive *mother's* inability
to conceive, without considering the possible consequences of
her adoptive father's infertility (see 1977, 32). This slant is not
incidental. As studies of involuntary childlessness have shown
(Miall 1986), the social position of women makes them more

likely than men to be subject to stigmatization. Although available medical data indicate that infertility is by no means only "the woman's problem," even physically fertile women tend to "accept perceived responsibility for the infertility" (277). More so than men, women are defined by their reproductive capabilities. By failing to become mothers, they have failed to become women (Ussher 1989, 100).

In the exclusive focus on women's infertility, which sustains the assumption that women's sexual and psychological adjustment is inherently related to childbearing, one can trace a persistent and deep-rooted essentialist image of women's nature. In her interviews with adoptees, Judith Modell (1994, 124) found that their descriptions of birth mothers often fit the cultural interpretation of mothers as "loving, emotionally giving, and sexual—productively sexual—whereas adoptive mothers more often were described as rigid and emotionally cold." It is impossible to know to what extent these descriptions were influenced by idealized images of motherhood, but there is enough research on the effects of stigmatization to suggest that such portrayals also serve as self-fulfilling prophecies. Perceptions do matter. Yet, by excluding the mediating force of stigmatization, search activists have proposed that the inability to bear children is inherently linked to negative personality traits and mental health problems. Cultural images of barren women are important conveyers of shared meanings. As such they are indispensable as rhetorical devices.

EXPERIENCE VERSUS EXPERTISE

I have so far said little about the arguments of those who oppose adoption reform, except to note the reciprocity of their moral vocabulary. Like the search activists, this group is far from monolithic. Nevertheless, some central themes characterize closed records rhetoric. Historically, arguments against open records have been synonymous with expert opinion, which has science as its ultimate truth referent. In his work on the culture of public problems, Joseph Gusfield (1981, 76–78) drew attention to the "dramatic significance of fact" in public debates. Facts portray the world as orderly, as cognitively as well as morally definite, and they are typically legitimated by science and mediated by numbers and statistics.

Like many other public controversies, the debate over adoption reform is also a dispute over facts and numbers. Not surprisingly, the statistics presented by search activists and those who oppose reform tend to diverge. As an example, the over-representation of adoptees in American psychiatric wards has been seen as an indicator of the psychological risks of secrecy in adoption. Amy Dean begins her book *Letters to My Birthmother* (1991, xiii) by citing a cover story in *Time* (Gibbs 1989) which claims that "adoptees represent 2% of the U.S. population, yet by some estimates they account for one-quarter of the patients in U.S. psychological treatment facilities." There is, however, no consensus on the actual number of adoptees who suffer from emotional problems or are under psychiatric care.

Another strategic statistic concerns the number of searchers. Opponents of reform, as I have noted, have claimed that "fewer than 1 percent" of adoptees and birth parents are interested in searching (Foster 1979, 36), that 95 percent are content with their lack of identifying information (see Churchman 1986, 11), and that searchers constitute "a minuscule minority" of adoptees (Zeilinger 1979, 47). Activists, on the other hand, have pointed to the growing number of grass-roots adoption-rights organizations and described their memberships as only "the tip of the iceberg" (Churchman 1986, 11). Because the search movement regards the desire to search as a universally present but often repressed human need, however, the actual number of searchers is not crucial to their claims.

Given that the very mandate of experts rests upon their claims to esoteric knowledge, the legitimacy of arguments advanced by adoption professionals has often been taken for granted, at least until the advent of the search controversy. In our society science stands as a metaphor for truth, and if an argument is held to be scientific, it is automatically assumed to be true. In the debate over adoption reform, the rationality and factuality of expert knowledge have been contrasted with the presumed irrationality and emotionality of the search activists' claims. Rather than being regarded as a source of insight and realism, a personal desire to search is viewed as a bias and an impediment—in any case, not as a sufficient truth claim. As one adoption professional (Foster 1979, 34) who opposed the disclosure of identifying information observed: "What is needed is a realistic discussion of the effects that opening adoption records would have. . . . Such a discussion cannot be obtained if a priori it has been decided that there is a right to know. . . . Therefore, let us simply discuss the advantages and disadvantages of open records without prejudging the matter."

As the sealed records policy has come under attack, so has adoption expertise, with past expert opinions having come under sharp criticism. Nonetheless, this challenge to what has been regarded as a final authority has not inhibited search activists themselves from relying on scientific references and expert opinions and from appealing to scientific rationality. Search groups distribute lists of scientific references that support the search (Adoptees-in-Search 1992), and prominent scientists and intellectuals (such as the father of sociobiology, Edward Wilson [Lifton 1988, 6]) lend authority to arguments in favor of open records. The most important argument in favor of the disclosure of identifying information about birth parents has been that knowledge of one's biological origins is necessary for the normal development of identity; this argument is based primarily on scientific theories of identity development (see Sachdev 1989, 12). Clearly, adoption experts' past mistakes have not reduced the search movement's reliance upon their social authority.

Because some of the most influential search activists are also clinically trained therapists, the distinction between activists and experts in the adoption debate is therefore not clear-cut. The close affinity between members of the search movement and cultural elites such as therapists, established authors, and journalists has clearly increased the voice of the movement and provided more cultural influence than it otherwise would have had.[12]

The readiness of both camps to embrace the "scientistic" mode of reasoning has some important consequences. "Scientism" entails "the conviction that we can no longer understand science as *one* form of possible knowledge, but rather must identify knowledge with science" (Habermas 1972, 4). Although search activists have rooted their critique of the American adoption system in the personal experiences of adoptees, science, including psychoanalytic theory, has remained the most authoritative legitimator of new realities in the sealed records debate (see Hubbard 1982, 19). This is unfortunate, since scientism is nourished by the close affinity of knowledge and power, dominant ideologies, and interpretations. Consequently the rules for truth in the area of adoption expertise have so far

12. For a discussion of this aspect of social movements, see McAdam (1994, 53–54).

excluded broader cultural considerations in favor of a decontextualizing, individualizing, and often depoliticizing approach to dilemmas of adoption.

Some research, such as studies of reunion outcomes (chap. 3), can surely be used to support adoptees' quest for genealogical knowledge. Yet the channeling of life stories through established therapeutic and scientific canons (such as particular identity theories) may be not necessarily a liberation but "a deliverance from one into another system of authority" (Rice 1992, 353). This is a risk especially when scientific research is used to make universal claims concerning human nature, without taking the social context of these experiences into account. Both adoption researchers and search-movement activists have tended to suppress differences *among* adoptees—that is, the heterogeneity of their social and psychological experiences. Although some components of adoption are shared by many adoptees, the insistence by the movement on a generic adoption experience—"*the* adoption experience" (Lifton 1988)— does not sufficiently recognize experiential diversity and positional meaning. Activist groups do need a unified collective and public identity to make effective strategic claims (Johnston, Laraña and Gusfield 1994, 18), but collective identities can also be overly restrictive and exclusionary and they may ultimately undermine the movement's goal by distancing potential members or protagonists. By drawing on and reinforcing the cultural stigma of adoption and infertility, the search movement risks doing just that.

5

Adoption in Popular Culture
SIMILAR YET DIFFERENT

I wasn't born in the sewer, you know . . . and like you I want some respect, a recognition of my basic humanity. But most of all, I want to find out who I am, by finding my parents, learning my human name, simple stuff that the good people of Gotham take for granted.
—The Penguin, *Batman Returns*

The considerable media attention given to adoption in the past two decades, in particular to issues surrounding the search, indicates that the adoption theme has meanings and connotations that capture the general public's interest. In the twelve months between April 1993 and March 1994, the adoption theme was featured 113 times in nationwide radio and TV news programs.[1] By comparison, other family-related topics, such as abortion and pregnancy, were featured more frequently (186 and 181 times, respectively); topics that were discussed less often include divorce and separation (97 times), birth control (31 times), and infertility (30 times). Considering the low number of adoptions relative to other family- or pregnancy-related issues, the popularity of the adoption topic is noteworthy.

For an audience that has little or no personal experience of adoption, the search serves as a compelling symbolic drama that both tests and clarifies their own, often unformulated questions concerning identity and the nature of family bonds. In a time

---

1. Topic Alert Hits are provided by Journal Graphics, Denver, 1994 and include the news programs of ABC, CNN, PBS, and NPR.

of high divorce rates and unstable relationships, media stories about adoptees and birth parents in search of their unknown biological relatives might function to calm deeply harbored anxieties about the meaning and strength of the blood relation.

Popular culture depicts adoptees and their quest for genealogical knowledge as familiar yet different: adoption stories are compelling to the extent that the audience can identify with them.[2] Yet, by placing adoptees firmly outside the order of nature, adoption is also a marker for difference. The media envisions the adoptee as the Other, and the search as potentially dangerous; consequently the audience's identification with the adoptee remains safe and detached. Like the Penguin in Tim Burton's *Batman Returns* (1992), adoptees can appeal to the public for sympathy in their quest for origins, yet in some sense they tend to remain freaks, to be pitied or even feared. Search activists have reinforced this dangerous and antisocial image of adoptees by prominently featuring in their writings "adoptees who kill," including some notorious serial killers (Lifton 1994, 87–108).

In this chapter I focus on representations of the search in contemporary popular culture, especially on television. Two well-known variations of the adoption theme—one in operatic form, the other in literary—are also analyzed. As an example of the representation of adoption in elite culture I have chosen the libretto from Richard Wagner's *Siegfried;* within the mass culture, I examine P. D. James's *Innocent Blood* and transcripts from recent television talk shows on the subject of searching. Despite their obvious differences, these three social texts all reveal an underlying structure that depicts adoption and the search as familiar yet also unnatural, pathological, and different.

2. As Munson (1993, 71) argues, it is a general feature of talk shows that they present topics that are both unusual and familiar to the audience.

The analysis of talk-show representations of adoption focuses on three aspects: the tension between the natural and the social elements of kinship, the authority of expert knowledge over personal experience, and the tendency to individualize dilemmas of adoption. The analysis in chapter 4 assumed that search activists have benefited from the widespread cultural conviction that the blood relation should not be violated. The analysis in this chapter shows that the public image of adoption and kinship is more complex and ambiguous than that. If we assume that a culture can be understood in terms of cognitive polarities or contradictions—what Kai Erikson (1976, 82) has called cultural "axes of variation"—images of adoption are better viewed in terms of a deep-rooted ambivalence regarding the nature of family bonds.

ADOPTION AS SYMBOLIC DRAMA

Siegfried: You lie, you loathsome loon!
   That the young look like their parents
   I've luckily seen for myself.
   When I came to the clear brook
   I saw the trees and beasts mirrored there;
   sun and clouds, just as they are,
   appeared reflected in the sparkling stream.
   There too I saw my own picture:
   quite unlike you I seemed to be;
   as like as a toad and a glittering fish;
   but a fish never had a toad for a father!
Mime: You are prating utter rubbish!
Siegfried: Look, now of my own accord
   it becomes clear to me
   what I've long pondered in vain:
   when I run into the forest to escape you,

how is it that I return?
From you I must first discover
who are my father and my mother?
Mime: What father? What mother?
Idle question!
Siegfried: Then I must seize you like this
to find out anything:
by gentleness I learn nothing!
I've had to force everything from you:
I'd scarcely have learnt even speech
had I not wrung it, rogue, from you by force!
Out with it, you shabby scoundrel!
Who are my father and my mother?
—Wagner, *Siegfried*

Few operatic works have been received as enthusiastically and generated such a dedicated following as Wagner's *Ring of the Nibelungen*. In *Ring of Power* (1993), the psychiatrist Jean Shinoda Bolen used the mythic material of the four *Ring* cycle operas to uncover and explain destructive family patterns. For the purpose of exploring the cultural symbolism of the adoption theme, the third opera, *Siegfried,* is the most interesting. It tells the story of a child, Siegfried, who, following the murder of his parents by the god Wotan, is raised by the dwarf Mime; although the dwarf knows the truth of the orphan's tragic past and the identity of his parents, he refuses to divulge it. As Bolen notes, Mime acts as Siegfried's martyr-mother, while Siegfried plays the part of the ungrateful adult-child. Mime sees himself as a devoted and unselfish parent and reacts to Siegfried's hostility by entangling him in "a web of need and guilt" (106). Although she interprets *Siegfried* not as an adoption story but as a story of family relationships in general, the patterns she uncovers are similar to some of the psychological dilemmas described in the literature on adoption and mental health (chap. 3). Indeed, according to some adoption experts and search activists, such patterns are characteristic of adoptive families and expose the underlying pathology of adoption. Bolen, however, does not share this individualistic psychomedical approach to family dysfunction but argues that problematic family relations cannot be resolved unless the larger social principles upon which these family patterns are based are changed as well.

Like many other heroic myths, *Siegfried* reflects the belief that environmental influences are mainly constraining and that true personal identity and self-fulfillment can be attained only by finding a natural core, by following one's intuition and overcoming social obstacles (see Snook 1973).

This ancient mythic theme of the orphan or foundling in search of her or his biological origins has many classic and contemporary equivalents. The list of well-known works in which this theme and the related themes of illegitimacy and orphanhood are elaborated includes Sophocles' *Oedipus Rex*, Shakespeare's *King Lear*, Mark Twain's *The Tragedy of Pudd'nhead Wilson*, George Bernard Shaw's *Major Barbara*, Charles Dickens's *Oliver Twist*, Anton Chekhov's *The Cherry Orchard*, Henry Fielding's *Tom Jones*, Edith Wharton's *The Old Maid*, and Edward Albee's *Tiny Alice* and *Who's Afraid of Virginia Woolf?* As Jenny Teichman noted, "Illegitimacy itself is the paradigm of a shameful secret and can symbolize all kinds of other secrets, deceptions and mysteries" (1982, 123); the adoption theme contains similar symbolic connotations. Albee, an adoptee himself, has used the adoption theme both overtly and covertly to insinuate secrecy and deception in many of his plays (see Glenn 1974).

In the professional community of scientists, as well as among the general public, adoption has served to clarify the importance of blood ties. For psychologists, adoption has provided a rare experiment in the relative impact of nature and nurture on the development of intelligence and other personality traits. Sociobiologist Daniel Freedman (1979, 21–23) has argued that the absence of biological ties in adoptive families makes a definitively negative difference in the quality of child rearing. Furthermore, he has interpreted adoptees' desire to search for the birth parents as evidence of the importance of genes or genetic connections in human behavior. Scientists have studied identical twins separated at birth in order to test the hereditarian theory of IQ, and adoptee studies of psychiatric disorders have been used to measure the genetic components of schizophrenia.[3] By drawing attention to pathological traits among adoptees, this line of research may have inadvertently added to the stigma of adoption, especially since the results have been widely reported in popular magazines such as *Psychology Today*.[4] Authors of literary fiction have employed the theme for similar purposes. In Maxwell Anderson's filmed adaptation of William March's novel *The Bad Seed*, for example, the adoption theme is used to promulgate the idea that criminal behavior—indeed, the will to evil—is inevitably hereditary (see Bailey 1957, 171–85).

BAD SEEDS AND INNOCENT BLOOD

Literature, though it may also be many other things, is social evidence and testimony. It is a continuous commentary on manners and morals. Its great monuments even as they address themselves

3. The scientific merits of these studies have been the focus of considerable dispute. See, for example, "Letters to the Editor" (1988, 875–76).
4. Despite the fact that the methodology of the adoption studies has been questioned (Lewontin, Rose, and Kamin 1984, 220–28).

to the eternal and existential problems which are at the root of the perennial tensions between men and their society, preserve for us the precious record of models of response to peculiar social and cultural conditions.

—Lewis Coser, *Sociology Through Literature*

The popularity of the adoption theme in the crime-mystery genre is hardly surprising. Mystery novels typically involve a struggle between good and evil and the presence of heroes, villains, and victims (Zola 1987, 486). P. D. James's *Innocent Blood* (1982) tells the story of an adopted woman in search of her biological origins. As in Wagner's mythical drama, the adoption theme in these mysteries serves a double function: it provides a formal structure for the mystery (that is, the search), and it carries cultural meanings that transcend the narrative itself. Search stories depict adoptees as similar yet different: similar to the extent that the reader identifies with the adoptee's yearning for identity, different to the extent that the adoptee is doomed to stand outside the natural order of things. Horror stories of the search (in literature as well as on talk shows) epitomize the similar-yet-different dilemma by empathizing with adoptees' desire to search yet also by portraying the search as dangerous and the truth as shocking.

An analysis of *Innocent Blood* illuminates the cultural images of adoption and their underlying structures of representation. In this story of a British adoptee in search of her biological origins, James captures the essential elements of the Western kinship mythology, a myth that pervades American society as well. Ironically the psychologists Michael and Heather Humphrey (1980, 43) note that "readers wanting a less academic introduction to the notion of genealogical bewilderment could do worse than begin here."

In *Innocent Blood*, Philippa Palfrey is an adoptee who upon reaching majority decides to take advantage of the British 1975 Children Act and embarks on a genealogical search. Here the distinction between the order of law and the order of nature could not be posited more clearly. Not only has Philippa been adopted, but she has been adopted by Maurice Palfrey, a renowned sociologist known for his writings on environmental influences on human development: "If he couldn't have a child of his own, at least he could rear one for the glory of sociological theory. It was surprising that he hadn't selected a second female, carefully matched for age and intelligence, to monitor their joint progress. After all, every experiment needed a control" (James 1982, 43).

Maurice Palfrey emerges as an unappealingly arrogant character whose discouraging response to Philippa's plans to search is reflected in his general dismissal of nature in favor of the man-made ("Maurice preferred buildings to nature, even nature as disciplined, organized, and formally displayed as Regent's Park" [219-20]). Her adoptive parents, as Philippa puts it, are "not exactly communicative" ("During a late dinner they sat like strangers; but strangers, after all, were what they were" [97]). The moral tale is made more complex by the fact that around the time of Philippa's adoption, her biological parents, as she will soon learn, were convicted for the rape and murder of a young girl. The story thus carries negative associations, implying danger both in the act of searching itself and in the immoral character of the biological parents.

Contending that the truth cannot be dismissed ("You're here because you're my mother. Nothing in life or death can alter that. It's the only thing about myself I can be sure of" [158]), Philippa decides to provide her birth mother with a home upon her release from prison. The women connect, yet the relationship remains curiously remote. In contrast to the rigid and warped personalities of the adoptive parents, which symbolize the unnatural, the birth mother belongs to the realm of nature, as symbolized by her love of roses, which is contrasted to the adoptive father's dislike for them and the adoptive mother's clumsiness in arranging them. Yet, after finally experiencing mother-daughter love ("It was all so easy, so beautifully easy. Why had it taken her so long to learn that there was nothing to afraid of in loving?" [291]), Philippa learns that her adoption was, after all, not the result of her biological parents' crime; she was adopted two weeks prior to the murder, because "there was no bonding of mother and child" (306).

Betrayed by the blood tie and the maternal instinct, Philippa returns to accuse the mother who deserted her, only to realize "that what bound her to her mother was stronger than hate or disappointment or the pain of rejection" (324). She returns, re-convinced of the primacy of nature, but too late; her mother has already committed suicide. As the result of a subplot, Philippa could be suspected of murdering her birth mother. Innocent as she is, she is free of official suspicion, but ironically it is her adoptive father, Maurice, the disbeliever in the blood tie, who finally cannot rid himself of the thought: "How long would it be before he could look into her eyes without wondering whether she was, after all, her mother's daughter, without asking himself whether she would have plunged that knife into a living throat?" (337). The hypocrisy of his insistence on the primacy of nurture having been revealed, the adoptive bond finally breaks down: the epilogue reveals a future sexual relationship between Philippa and Maurice, "an obstacle ceremoniously moved out of the way so that they could again take up their roles of father and daughter" (348).

Innocent Blood establishes the primacy of the order of nature on many levels. Not only is the relationship to the adoptive parents portrayed as strained and unnatural, but the adoptive parents' unflattering personalities are partly explained in terms of their childlessness, their inability to conceive. Although there are indications that Philippa's character resembles her adoptive father's, the final incestuous scene indicates that this resemblance is hardly that of father and daughter but rather that of two unrelated but similar individuals. Furthermore, in contrast to Phillipa's shocking but nevertheless genuine relationship to her birth mother, the life of the adoptive family is saturated by lies and secrets: "Whoever I am, nothing of me comes from Maurice and Hilda. How could it? They've done nothing but provide the props for this charade, the clothes, the artifacts" (50).

Yet the story also contains elements of contrast. By depicting adoptive family life as essentially false and the search as essentially dangerous, *Innocent Blood* succinctly summarizes the two most common cultural stereotypes about adoption. The plot suggests inherent dangers in the process of searching ("the shocking truth"), as well as in the sinful, even evil nature of the birth parents. This impression is further underscored by the concealed true reason for Philippa's abandonment, which James presents as almost more shocking than the murder, thereby suggesting that the abandonment of one's own child is more condemnable than the killing of somebody else's. The biological mother's final suicide generates little surprise or emotion but seems almost a natural solution to the unnatural crime of abandonment. Although this portrayal of adoptive family life highlights the sharp division between the order of nature and the order of law, the story also occasionally contrasts Philippa's sense of lack of attachment with Maurice's and Hilda's actual affection for her. In the end, however, with the revelation that the attachment between Maurice and Philippa is of a sexual nature, the primacy of nature is further accentuated.

James's depiction is in this respect consistent with the adoption laws in the United States, which do not regard a sexual union or marriage between adoptive relatives incestuous, a legal decision indicating that adoptive kinship is still not considered equivalent to consanguineal kinship. Although an increasing number of studies have pointed to the social rather than biological origins of the incest taboo, state courts have continued to rule that state laws on incestuous marriages apply only to blood relatives (Kirk 1985, 104-05). In popular culture as well as in social policy, the nature of adoptive bonds remains ambiguous.

The Search Movement and the Media

Media attention is crucial to the cultural influence of contemporary social movements (Gusfield 1994, 71), both in their early agenda-setting stages and for their later political success (see, e.g., Johnson 1989). On the one hand, the mass media "provide a series of arenas in which symbolic contests are carried out among competing sponsors of meaning" (Gamson and Stuart 1992). On the other hand, the media play an active role in interpreting and framing the movement's agenda (Gusfield 1994, 71), typically in a way that supports larger hegemonic structures (Gitlin 1979). In the case of the adoption reform movement, the media have raised and shaped public consciousness concerning adoptees' desire to search and have also contributed to the growth of the movement by fostering awareness among adoptees themselves. Studies of adoptees' attitudes toward searching have shown that publicity in the media has been a major factor promoting curiosity about their birth parents (Sachdev 1989, 84).

Although the search movement has benefited from the media's interest in adoption stories, activists do not control media representations of adoption. Constructionist studies of social problems have showed that public perceptions are shaped by the ways reporters frame or select stories.[5] Public disclosures of personal experiences are problematic, because they invite expert mediators to interpret and present experiences in terms of dominant norms and individualize the causal agent so that the human-interest element is dramatized while possible structural causes and solutions remain hidden (Gitlin 1979; Johnson 1989).

Adoption has been a newsworthy subject for four decades, but the slants have varied over time. Articles written during the 1950s usually offered advice to prospective adoptive parents. Issues of interracial adoption, single-parent adoption, and the adoption of special-needs children emerged for the first time in the early 1960s and were featured with increasing frequency in popular magazines toward the end of the decade. Other new adoption issues of the late 1960s concerned the "baby shortage" and the "baby market," topics that continued to be debated throughout the next two decades. Although issues of secrecy in adoption were discussed during the 1950s and 1960s, the debate concerned not access to identifying information but rather whether adoptees should be told about the adoption in the first place ("Keep Adoption a Secret" 1960; Whitmore 1959).

In 1974, the disclosure of adoption records became a topic in its own right. Although adoptees' need for information about birth parents had been examined occasionally ("Why Did My Mother Give Me Away?" 1965), it was not until the mid-1970s that such psychological quandaries were related to the social and legal issue of disclosing adoption records. Many of the first articles on this topic were written by prominent search activists

5. In the late 1970s sociologists studying social problems shifted their emphasis away from the conditions that cause the "problems" to the process whereby certain conditions are defined as socially problematic (Schneider 1985).

(e.g., Lifton 1976). In the early 1980s, a new type of adoption story emerged: the reunion narrative. Although reunions between adoptees and their birth parents were not new, in the 1980s they became a focus of media attention, with magazines running articles carrying dramatic titles such as "Blood Is Thicker Than Surnames: Reunion of Adopted Triplets" (1988) and "I Gave My Daughter Away—and Found Her Again" (Hudgens 1980). Reunion narratives have also made the experiences of birth parents more visible. Their virtual invisibility in the media before the 1970s reflected the powerlessness of birth parents, especially birth mothers, within the adoption system. The new interest in reunions signals, if not a complete shift in power, at least increased sympathy for unwed mothers.

The sealed records issue continues to be the focus of considerable debate, but it has recently given way to some extent to new adoption-related issues, most notably the adoption by Americans of infants from Eastern Europe and the well-publicized custody cases of "Gregory K." and "Baby Jessica." These cases are not part of the sealed records debate, but media coverage of them illustrates that beyond their use-value in eliciting extreme emotions, there is little agreement concerning the relative importance of nature and nurture in family relationships and the meaning of the "child's best interests."

Adoption on Talk Shows: Familiar Yet Different

Television is a key mechanism in the production of an ideologically uniform mass culture. Although individuals interpret meanings differently, depending on their experience and place in society, television has the power to reflect and create a certain degree of ideological uniformity (Lewis 1991, 6). Television remains the primary source of "shared stories," which explain "life as an American to those holding the dominant vision in the culture as well as to a large number outside that dominant vision in some way" (Condit 1990, 123; Thornburn 1987).[6]

The argumentative quality of the talk show is well suited to reveal dilemma-ridden aspects of ideology and culture. Although the pursuit of controversy on such programs is planned or controlled to a considerable degree (Tuchman 1974, 130), the format nevertheless allows contrasts and tensions to surface. For the purpose of sociological analysis, not only talk shows but other television dramas as well can serve as "a kind of theater in which certain contrary tendencies are played out" (Erikson 1976, 82). A revealing example of the cultural tension between the biological and social aspects of kinship or parent-child bonding is provided by George Gerbner (1988, 3), who found in his study of media portrayals of adoption that the number of adoptees engaged in a search for their birth parents on television dramas was about ten to eighteen times higher than the percentage of adoptees who search in real life. Yet, while the focus on searching suggests an interest in blood ties, the plot resolutions of these dramas generally upheld "the reality and the strength of the adoptive bond" (4). The tension between the biological and social aspects of kinship and parent-child bonding is, of course, not confined to media discourse but crucially affects those most intimately affected by adoption.

6. Like the mass media in general, the talk show serves as a "boundary-maintaining mechanism" that establishes a "discourse of the normal" (Munson 1993, 83). It also provides "a sort of testing ground for changing social mores (Rapping 1987, 135), a narrative "in which society's central beliefs and values undergo continuous rehearsal, testing and revision" (Thornburn 1987, 161). In the talk-show setting argumentation and disputation are routine activities, and the show is typically structured as a "pursuit of controversy" (Hutchby 1992, 673).

Search activists often appear as guests on talk shows examining adoption, and the discussions understandably reflect the agenda of the movement. Underscoring the involuntary and coercive nature of the adoption process, birth mothers are typically described as women who have "surrendered" or "lost children to adoption." Genealogical information is described as necessary for the adoptee "to be complete" (*Geraldo* 1988a, 8; 1991a, 12), and the missing child or birth parent is compared to "a missing piece" (*Donahue* 1986, 13), a missing "part of your body" (*Sally Jessy Raphael* 1991, 8). Consider the following excerpt from an Oprah Winfrey show entitled "Holiday Reunions for Separated Families":

Oprah: So, when you started the search, you were looking for a piece of yourself, as Robert said?

Ms. Plocek: Yes, I married a blue-eyed blond. My children look like my husband. So, I never had anyone that resembled me. I didn't know much about my past, my background. I just wanted—there was a little piece of me missing and I wanted to put that piece back in place. I have wonderful parents, a wonderful sister, but it still didn't—still something was missing. A little something was missing.

Oprah: . . . and so you go through life feeling a little incomplete?

Ms. Plocek: A little.

Oprah: You know, like a kneecap is off or something, yeah, yeah. (*Oprah* 1990, 7)

To emphasize the biological constituents of kinship, physical resemblance is often emphasized. In the following excerpt, parent-child bonding is described in exclusively biological terms:

Mr. Montague: I knew it was her before she told me who she was.

Donahue: Really? Uh-huh. We believe you. I'm sure it's that primal. (*Donahue* 1989, 9)

Similarities in taste and preference are also introduced as evidence for the natural basis of kinship, as in the following excerpt from a *Donahue* broadcast on the reunion of twins separated at birth (1986, 4). This aspect of kinship based on biology serves as the introduction to a more general discussion of searching and the disclosure of birth records:

Anthony: The first night in Miami we shared a room together. Roger didn't want to go to his mother's house because he wanted some hours to spend together, bring up personal things. We discovered when we were unpacking our bag that we used the same type of hair lotion, which at the time was Vitalis. He says look, Tony, I use Vitalis too.
Audience: (Laughter)
Anthony: At the time we both smoked, we no longer smoke. We both smoked Lucky Strikes at the time. We both discovered that we used a toothpaste called Vatamakup, a Swedish brand toothpaste which—really, it was incredible. I couldn't believe that he had the same type of toothpaste.

Yet, although talk-show representations of adoption and searching in many ways reinforce the primacy of the blood tie over the social aspects of parent-child bonding, counterthemes do appear. Although the wish to search for birth parents and children given up for adoption is justified by the numerous references to the significance of blood ties, an equally popular approach to the issue of disclosure is the situation in which an adoptee or a birth parent has been contacted by a biological relative against his or her will. Whereas search activists depict birth mothers as "women who have lost children to adoption" (*Geraldo* 1988a, 8), adoptees who oppose change blame "head-hunting agencies" and the birth parents for "hunting them down" and thereby violating their right to privacy (*Sally* 1991, 8). Such adoptees are likely to ask: "But what about my rights? You took all that away from me. Nobody asked me if I wanted to see you" (*Sally* 1991, 4).

Competing conceptions of kinship and parent-child bonding surface, particularly in discussions about motherhood. Search activists stress the natural basis of pregnancy, childbirth, and motherhood, whereas those who oppose disclosure define motherhood as social in character. Examples abound: "Giving birth to a child does not make you a mother or a father" or "Raising a child . . . and loving it and taking care of it makes you its mother. Biological birth doesn't mean a thing" (*Donahue* 1989, 11; 1991, 21); "Giving birth to a child does not make you a mother or a father" or "She is the woman who gave birth to her. That does not make her mother" (*Sally* 1991, 21, 16). The same tension characterizes definitions of love. When an audience member on *Donahue* argues that "love is not biological" (*Donahue* 1991, 21) or when Geraldo claims that "love is what counts" (*Geraldo* 1988b, 11), he or she simultaneously refutes the view that blood ties are enough to make a family.

In his study of talk-show culture, Wayne Munson (1993, 80) argues that the talk show erodes the elitist "culture of expertise" by dispersing knowledge among guests, experts, and the host. According to Munson, the talk show both upholds democratic principles and discloses a crisis of authority in contemporary American society; this applies to talk-show representations of searching. For example, in a discussion on *Sonya Live* (1992, 7) regarding the legitimacy of sealed records, a caller challenges the expertise of Dr. William Pierce, president of the National Council for Adoption, which advocates mutual consent rather than disclosure upon demand:

1st Caller: I'm an adoptee and have read a lot of Mr. Pierce's articles, and I don't know what makes the man an expert, since he has probably not been adopted himself to know this feeling of an adoptee. And I do believe it's every American's right to know their birthright, no matter how it turns out in the end.

By allowing the caller to question the guest's monopoly on expert knowledge, the host invites him to proclaim the superiority of his lived experience over Pierce's more formal credentials. Yet most shows on searching feature experts as representatives of reason, including search activists who are trained as therapists or social workers and who draw upon their position as experts to give added credence to the legitimacy of their claims. Geraldo (1991b, 11) introduced one guest this way:

Randy Rolfe is a parent-child counselor. She's the author of the book *Adult Children Raising Children*. She is a therapist-counselor in private practice in Philadelphia. We're going to get some input from her to hopefully bring some sanity to this discussion.

One common way to reinforce the superiority of expert knowledge is to allow the expert to summarize the discussion, to get the last word. The epistemological tension between experience and theory, emotions and knowledge, subjectivity and objectivity, also applies to shows in which members of the search movement are granted expert status in their questioning of nonsearchers' feelings and intentions. Although the search movement has emphasized the importance of trusting lived experience, occurrences that do not fit preestablished truths are called into doubt:

3d Caller: . . . You had asked whether or not some children have a yearning need to find out who their real parents are. In my case, I do not wish to know. I was adopted, and I think that it would be unfair and an intrusion in my life and my adoptive parents', who are my only parents in my eyes. I think it would be completely unfair to them and myself. My real parents, or biological parents made a decision 24 years ago, and they also stand by that.

Sonya: Now, Lisa, stay on the phone with us, 'cause I'd like you to meet Betty Jean Lifton, who found her birth parents years ago, now focuses on adoption in her psychotherapy practice, and is the author of *Journey of the Adopted Self, A Quest for Wholeness.* [Interviewing:] How would you respond to Lisa?

Betty Jean Lifton: I think Lisa sounds like someone who grew up in a closed adoption system. And that is: the child is told from a very early age that, "These are your parents, and you're not to think about your other family." And a child has a lot of divided loyalty and learns to repress his or her thoughts and questions.

Sonya: So what she's doing is bad, bad for her?

Lifton: Well, she's doing what's natural for her, because if you grow up in a closed system, this is the way you sound. And she hasn't yet been in touch with her—I say—her unconscious. But you could say she hasn't yet awakened to her rights and her needs as a person. Do you think that's true, Lisa? You're not awakened to your needs? Let's stay out of rights for a moment.

3d Caller: No, not at all. I feel that I am very comfortable in the fact that I was adopted. I have no bad feelings about it whatsoever, and I'm so comfortable with the parents that I have and feel so loved. (*Sonya* 1994, 4)

Without necessarily refuting the accuracy of psychoanalytic inquiry or the possibility that the caller has in fact repressed her wish to know, this example shows that it is still the expert (in this case a member of the search movement) who deciphers the confession and limits the discourse of truth. At the same time that speech is encouraged, a "policing of statements" occurs as the expert scrutinizes the "raw data of the confessor's speech for signs of pathology" (Alcoff and Gray 1993, 271). In the above example, although the caller denies the accuracy of the expert's statement, the discourse of the normal is established by the expert in such a way that a refusal to confess is taken as further proof of pathology, and the caller is thus denied authority and agency.

As Linda Alcoff and Laura Gray noted in their Foucauldian analysis of survivor discourse, the confessional mode used in talk shows might at first appear to give the speaker an empowering permission, even incitement, to speak about her or his inner feelings and griefs. Yet there are several dangers associated with public confessions. They have the potential to become media commodities, with use-value determined primarily on the basis of nationalism and drama. How else could we understand Geraldo's focus on adoptees seduced by their birth parents (*Geraldo* 1991b)? As in *Innocent Blood*, the dramatic thrust of this *Geraldo* segment is heightened by the portrayal of both the search and the biological parents as dangerous. The label of illegitimacy marks adoptees as different. Although many talk-show hosts are supporters of the search movement and advertise search groups such as ALMA on their programs, public reunions and confessions are not intended to convey subtlety and caution; as media commodities they are valued primarily as public spectacles and for their capacity to elicit emotions.

A second problem with the confessional mode, according to Alcoff and Grey, is that it draws attention to the psychological states of individuals but neglects to address external sources of distress. In subtle and not so subtle ways, adoptees' motives for searching are questioned and individualized: "Is [your search] driven at all by dissatisfaction with your adoptive parents?" (*Sonya* 1994, 1). Reflecting a more general tendency in the media to individualize and decontextualize social issues (see, e.g., Johnson 1989), the causal agents are typically defined as corrupt adoption agencies (*Geraldo* 1988b, 9), possessive adoptive parents, and misguided social workers, whereas more far-reaching systemic causes (including the reasons adoptions are necessary in the first place) go unexamined. Inequalities perpetuated by the adoption system are virtually never recognized as part of a broader pattern of class or gender inequality. The adoptive parents' reactions to reunions are seldom understood as the psychological effects of social stigmatization. Reluctance to take part in the talk-show confessional is itself perceived as a sign of dishonesty or repression:

Sonya: Now, Jack, we did invite your adopted mother to participate in this discussion. She declined our invitation. I don't want to read anything to that that's not there, but I would have to say that I found that interesting and wondered if it's a point of conflict for her. (*Sonya* 1992, 4)

It is not only the adoptive parents whose behavior and opinions have been explained in terms of individual shortcomings and character traits. Some shows on dramatic and involuntary reunions portray the tactlessness or selfishness of individual adoptees and birth parents as the source of the problem. Dilemmas of adoption are typically framed as individual problems that can be resolved by altering individual behavior patterns and attitudes, by recognizing or discovering one's true desires. The *Donahue* audience reproaches a biological mother who does not wish to meet her child: "How can you not have any emotion at all and be so cold?" (*Donahue* 1991, 25).

The Search Debate and the Fate
of the American Family

I think this is a very emotional program and I'm, you know, an admirer of your program. And of all the things that are happening here today, I think this is one of the best programs I ever seen in my life.
—Audience member, *Geraldo*

Some distinctively American preoccupations have contributed to the popularity of the adoption theme. As numerous observers have noted, the American ideology of the self reflects the "myth of 'starting over' without the weight of origins" (Ginsburg 1989, 221). The comparatively early institutionalization of adoption in the United States has been explained in terms of the widely accepted notion that "man was not simply born into his rank but created his own place in the world" (Shalev 1989, 38). The same argument has been evoked in support of the sealed records policy, which has been said to reflect "the American emphasis on individual responsibility and achievement" (Foster 1979, 37). At least in part, the resistance to greater openness in adoption reflects the strength of the belief that one creates rather than inherits one's identity (36). A slightly different version of the same argument was recently suggested in a *New Yorker* editorial (Comment 1993, 7):

> The United States might be said to have a special interest in the maintenance and repair of adoption: metaphorically, at least, adoption is what made America great, for America's very nationhood is

adoptive. . . . And, while we honor old ties, a sub-
stantial part of our very identity consists in the
ability to transcend them with new ones—in the
power that the heart has over the blood.

Not only the defenders of the sealed records policy but also
search activists have evoked the ideal of individualism in order
to justify their claims. As I have noted, the argument for adoption reform has often been phrased in terms of the ethic of
self-discovery, which elevates the idea of finding oneself to a
moral duty. U.S. adoption policy and the current debate reflect
the belief that identity, like destiny, is achieved, not ascribed.

Images of adoption are inevitably and intimately interwoven
with perceptions and fears of the fate of the mainstream family.
The rise of the search narrative as the most popular type of
adoption story in American mass media during the past decade
is not coincidental but mirrors a contemporary anxiety over the
fate of the family and the strength of kinship bonds. In their
comparison of adoption in the United States and Great Britain,
H. David Kirk and Susan A. McDaniel (1984, 78) noted that
U.S. adoption policy to a much greater extent "enshrines an
anachronistic image of the family, nostalgically regarded as the
core of true and good family organization and relationships."
The reluctance of American adoption professionals and legislators to open adoption files, they claim, can be traced to an un-
recognized attempt to "prop up this idealization" of the family.
They explain this tendency as a culturally specific response to
weakened family ties, propelled by a general insecurity over the
cohesion of American society: a society "surer of its past" would
have "less need of idealized culture images and values."[7]

This persistent focus on idealized images of the family illuminates the current public preoccupation with adoption as well.

7. In contrast, the opening of British adoption records in 1975 is "in-

For the past two decades, conservative as well as liberal commentators have debated the decline of the American family. Among other things, these commentators have expressed concern over the rising divorce rate and the increasing number of single-parent households; they have questioned the erosion of the family's autonomy by the state (see Skolnick 1991). The public interest in adoption is directly linked to these concerns. By reinforcing belief in the strength of blood ties, media stories about adoptees and birth parents in search of unknown biological relatives serve to calm anxieties over the presumed erosion of the family. The yearly holiday reunions between birth parents and adoptees on *Oprah*, for example, attest to the importance of blood ties in times of family breakdown. According to Norval Glenn (1991, 669), "As marriage and other heterosexual pair-bonding becomes less secure, the relations of adults to 'blood' kin, especially ascendant and descendant kin, may become more important, both in the lives of individuals and to the functioning of society." Adoptees' insistence on their legal and moral right to know their biological kin thus reinforces the trust in the blood tie that Americans have come to doubt.

---

dicative of a society surer of its past and less in need of idealized cultural images and values" (Kirk and McDaniel 1984, 133).

6

Conclusion

ADOPTION IN CONTEXT

[Activists]—along with everyone else—are attracted to simplifying categories, maintaining unconscious attachments to stereotypes, and thinking within contested versions of reality that tend to treat some realities as more valid than others.
—Martha Minow, *Making All the Difference*

In this book, the concept of difference has been used mostly to question the depiction of adoptees as different—that is, as pathological Others—but also to criticize the search movement's suppression of differences among adoptees, its unwillingness to recognize the varying experiences of growing up adopted. The quest by adoptees for genealogical knowledge is part of the "new cultural politics of difference" that has surfaced during the past two decades among marginalized social groups, especially women, ethnic and racial minorities, and gays and lesbians (West 1990). These groups have formed social movements that challenge dominant cultural representations of them as inferior and lacking, and they have infused their difference with positive rather than negative meanings. Suffice it to repeat in this context that representations of adoption and adoptees in contemporary American society (in research as well as in popular culture) tend to reflect the assumption that blood ties determine our feelings of kinship and sense of identity and that adoptees and adoptive families therefore are inherently pathological and deficient (Nelkin and Lindee 1995).

Yet, in their attempt to redefine for themselves and others

what it means to be adopted, search activists have in some respects solidified society's negative views of adoptive kinship, in particular as applied to definitions of motherhood and identity. The type of strategic action that characterizes modern social movements typically involves "a stylized and planned staging of one's identity for the purpose of gaining recognition and/or influence" (Cohen 1985, 706-07). Such staging of a group's common identity is often linked to the overturning or reversal of stereotypes, both as a political goal and as an incentive to political activism. The pursuit of social change, however, does not make critics or reformers immune to repeating "in new contexts a version of the old assumptions they set out to contest" (Minow 1990, 229). Activists share with their opponents and their audience the human propensity to categorize and simplify, and they have furthermore "internalize[d] scripts about how to argue, and indeed, how to know" (232-39).

As search activists have argued, there has been a tendency among lobbyists who oppose open records to polarize the debate and to label search activists "anti-adoption" (Lifton 1994, 8). Yet, search activists have also polarized the debate by refusing to consider seriously the views of adoptees who do not wish to search. Moreover, rather than challenging the negative cultural representation of adoption, the search movement has tended to use popular but stigmatizing portrayals of adoptees and their families, adoptive mothers in particular. This rhetorical strategy not only conforms to society's negative stereotypes of adoption and adoptive motherhood but caters to a general tendency in American society to blame mothers, an attitude that has been magnified by mental health experts, who have not explored how the behavior of mothers is shaped by social forces.[1]

1. As Caplan argues in *Don't Blame the Mother: Mending the Mother-Daughter Relationship* (1985, 39-67), there is a tendency among mental

The search movement's attempt to establish a new definition of "the adoption experience" has also tended to homogenize adoptees. So far, the movement has not contextualized adoption and the desire to search. In *Journey of the Adopted Self,* Lifton (1994, 129) writes that "the difference between those who search and those who don't lies in how they formed their defensive structures as children: how much they denied, repressed, and split off." This explanation is not necessarily inaccurate, but it is narrow and partial. Differences in the desire to search are also linked to real differences in experience and context, and one must allow for the possibility that some adoptees do not regard their biological origins as essential to their sense of self. Furthermore, the repression hypothesis draws on the assumption that biological ties are paramount, but it overlooks the extent to which the meaning of the blood relation is socially constructed. A more powerful argument for opening adoption records would *emphasize* the cultural context of adoption: since American society places so much emphasis on blood ties, it is both inconsistent and unfair to deny this information to adoptees who want it.

The Sealed Records Debate and the Social Construction of Mothering

Definitions of motherhood are central to the sealed records debate. Women constitute the majority of members of both adoptee and birth-parent self-help groups. The feminist critique of motherhood as a patriarchal institution can help expand the rights of adoptees and birth mothers by exposing the ideological sources of the systematic mistreatment of mothers

---

health experts to blame mothers for their children's problems without taking the mother's life situation and limited resources into account.

who do not conform to the American family ideal (Andersen 1991, 235–36)—for example, by giving birth out of wedlock. In the social welfare system, women themselves rather than men serve as the agents of social and patriarchal control. As Paula Dressel (1987, 295) has noted, "Welfare work is a female-dominated occupation undergirded by patriarchal ideologies," with regard to its content. In spite of the presence of women as both workers and clients, however, women's issues are not addressed (Rojek, Peacock, and Collins 1988, 77–113). With regard to the adoption process in particular, the role of female social workers is decidedly double-edged: although most adoption work is, and has been, inspired by humanitarian motives, adoption workers' treatment of birth and adoptive mothers has been shaped by patriarchal norms and assumptions about "good mothering." Adoption policies have also been shaped by social workers' attempts to gain authority and professional influence in a society that traditionally devalues women's work.

Feminists have been quick to support the right of both adoptees and birth mothers to search, pointing out that the sealed records policy has belittled the experience of pregnancy and birth and perpetuated patriarchal control over women's sexuality (Chesler 1989; Shalev 1989; Rothman 1989). In a patriarchal society, failure to fulfill social norms and ideals of motherhood has traditionally been regarded as a primary indicator of a woman's moral irresponsibility and social ineptitude, and women who have been categorized as bad or unfit mothers have been punitively affected by adoption policies. Yet, much like the nineteenth-century feminists who embraced the strategy of emphasizing biological difference and separate spheres, search advocates—including some feminists—have reinforced an ideology of mothering that reproduces confining stereotypes about adoption. With the notable exception of Barbara Katz Rothman (1989), feminists have largely failed to recognize the problematic situation of adoptive mothers from the perspective of gender. Gender domination has been considered crucial for understanding the predicament of birth mothers, while the situation of adoptive mothers has been seen as determined primarily by class. Although adoptive mothers, because of their economic and racial privilege, have seemingly benefited from class-biased adoption practices, their lives and experiences have also been circumscribed by normative assumptions about what constitutes good mothering. For example, some adoption agencies are still reluctant to allow couples to adopt if the wife "plan[s] to continue her career" (Kadushin and Martin 1988, 547). In this way, the agencies have not only contributed to the class bias of adoption practice (since the adoptive father's income under these circumstances must be high enough to support the household) but also reinforced a strict gender-based division of labor in the family. Ironically, this is a domestic ideal that most adoption workers themselves do not live up to. The experience of adoptive motherhood is also crucially shaped by age and heterosexist biases, which make it difficult for men and women who are single, over forty, or homosexual to adopt.

Perhaps the failure to problematize the situation of adoptive mothers reflects the recent reevaluation of motherhood in feminist thinking and scholarship (Hamilton 1990; Maroney 1990). For feminists, motherhood has provided a "prime site" for exploring and contesting the "boundaries of nature and culture," biology and identity. Whereas some researchers have challenged the natural as socially constructed, others have reaffirmed the concept of naturalness and viewed motherhood as an important site of political praxis (Glenn 1994, 1–19; Rowbothman 1989, 81–93). Some feminists have emphasized the importance of acknowledging women's lived experiences of childbearing without lapsing into essentialism; others have interpreted these attempts as a "reversion to an essentialist view of femininity as defined by biology, by the ability to bear children" (Rapping 1990). In her critique of scientific theories of mother-infant bonding, Diane Eyer (1992, 181) noted that although many feminists have been suspicious of biological explanations for women's behavior, the idea that there are biological under-pinnings to the mother-infant relationship fits in with the growing feeling that everything should be "natural"; feminists therefore have tended to endorse the "ideology of the natural."

The reevaluation of the naturalness of motherhood has cre-ated a tension within the feminist response to the sealed records debate. As Rothman (1989, 126) has poignantly argued, how-ever, the adoption process need not be perceived as a zero-sum game: "We can acknowledge the ongoing grief of a woman who has given up a baby without saying that makes her the real mother, or more the mother than the adoptive mother or father who gives ongoing love and care." The definition of kinship as genetic rather than social ultimately neglects the significance of nurturing. It is this same logic that has allowed the birth mother's experience of pregnancy and the trauma of loss to be discounted and that has drawn the distinction between legiti-mate and illegitimate children—a senseless distinction from the viewpoint of women's experience. This is not the same as to deny all significance of biological factors in human life and de-velopment, but it does question the primary significance of bi-ology for human attachment. It seems that in order to develop a more balanced understanding of adoption, motherhood, and kinship, feminists must seriously consider the predicament of both birth and adoptive mothers. Because the dominant bio-logical definition of motherhood takes the "adult woman = mother" equation for granted (Letherby 1994, 527) and as-sumes that women's mental health and maturity are inherently linked to the biological capacity to reproduce, it also misrep-resents women who are not mothers. The feminist response to the search movement's claim that adoption is an inherently oppressive institution has also so far left unanswered the question of whether birth mothers necessarily are always (directly or indirectly) forced to choose the adoption option, or whether adoption can *ever* serve the birth mother's best interests.

FALSE ALTERNATIVES: ABORTION AND ASSISTED REPRODUCTION

Two issues concerning human reproduction have relevance for the future of adoption: the debate over fetal rights versus women's right to abortion and the debate over ethical issues in assisted reproduction. In both instances, adoption has been endorsed as a preferable alternative. Furthermore, the issues raised in the sealed records debate are very similar to the questions concerning access to information about genetic origins that stem from the use of donated semen and eggs. These comparisons are misleading, however, to the extent that they are based upon similar unstated assumptions that perpetuate rather than abolish existing social inequalities in the sphere of reproduction.

When talk about family values became a standard component of the political rhetorical repertoire, during the Reagan and Bush campaigns and administrations, the practice of adoption gained political endorsement to an unprecedented extent. By calling adoption "the forgotten option" and establishing a White House Task Force on Adoption, Reagan became the first president to actively endorse adoption as an alternative to abortion. The adoption option provided a solution for the pro-life movement, which had been accused of showing more concern for the fetus than for the child, while also complementing the Republican administration's distaste for state intervention in matters of welfare. To quote a supporter of Reagan's policy, adoption "replaces expensive and impersonal government social programs with the devoted love and resources of permanent parents" (Chapman 1989, 27). Adoption advocates were quick to take advantage of their newfound political support. In 1989, adoption lobbyists used the possibility that the Supreme Court might decide to limit or even rescind women's right to abortion as the impetus to seek federal support for adoption (see, e.g., *Wall Street Journal* 1989). Antiabortion groups such as the evangelical De Moss Foundation initiated paid television campaigns that posed adoption as the "humane" alternative to abortion. During his presidential race and his tenure in the White House, Bush endorsed adoption as a solution to a number of family issues, such as teenage pregnancy and abortion. However, since the administration did not follow through on its promise of support for adoption (in fact, cuts in health and human services during this period led to diminished financial support for adoption), Bush's endorsement of the adoption option appears to have been intended primarily to defuse the abortion rights movement. Because those who would suffer most from abortion restrictions are poor and minority women, the children born as a result of such restrictions would most likely become the so-called hard-to-adopt.

There is no guarantee that the use of adoption as an alternative to abortion would change the situation of birth mothers in any way. To the contrary, by ignoring the fact that more and more poor women would be obliged to give up their babies for adoption for economic reasons, the development would intensify existing gender, class, and racial inequalities in adoption. Moreover, the National Committee for Adoption (1989, 108) has opposed "open adoption records because the confidentiality guarantee can be the deciding factor in a woman's abortion or adoption decision." Recent endorsements of the adoption option have assumed (but not proved) that women will not refrain from having abortions unless they are promised complete confidentiality in the adoption process. Given this stance, the chances of overturning the sealed records policy seem slight.

The new reproductive technologies and methods of assisted reproduction have been criticized from various points of view. Critics have argued, for example, that parents' desire to produce genetic offspring is less morally legitimate than the desire to nurture—"a sort of rhinoplasty for the ego" (Lauritzen 1993, 135); the desire to nurture, they claim, is more properly fulfilled by adoption. In addition, adoption generates social and economic benefits for the community; gamete donation does not. Others, again, have argued that the model of adoption to which donor insemination has been compared is more an outmoded myth than a reality and that a comparison that favors adoption is therefore misleading. Many of the same problems that critics attribute to assisted reproduction, such as the commercialization of reproduction and the commodification of children, characterize some contemporary adoption practices as well (125).

Although this observation seems correct to some extent—a recent overview of adoption (Flango 1990) refers to states as either net "importers" or net "exporters" of adoptable children —the comparison does not invalidate the argument in favor of adoption. By pointing out similarities between the traditional practice of adoption and the new reproductive methods, feminist observers have in this respect provided a more helpful and consistent critique (Rothman 1989, 126). It has been argued that all types of assisted reproduction give precedence to the genetic tie and that some types reinforce "the patriarchal focus on the seed as the source of being" (35). Yet, as noted, many feminist critics have accepted the primacy of the biological bond. Although they have warned against the ways the new reproductive technologies might further weaken women's role in a male-dominated gender order, the insistence by some feminists (such as Phyllis Chesler) on the centrality of the biological bond makes it difficult to see why women would not choose to undergo even costly, painful, and uncertain infertility treatments.

The debate concerning the right of individuals conceived by gamete donation to receive information about their genetic origins or donors has consequences for the debate over openness in adoption. Although anonymity is still the norm in both adoption and assisted reproduction, a move toward greater openness in cases of gamete donation will probably affect the future of the sealed records policy, and vice versa. Still, parallel developments cannot be taken for granted. In Great Britain, adoptees were granted the right to receive identifying information in 1975, but the issue of access to genetic information in the case of gamete donation has still not been fully resolved, although the 1990 Human Fertilization and Embryology Act stated that at least the "means of conception" cannot be kept a secret (Haimes 1992). Yet an increased awareness of the identity problems of donor-inseminated children and adults will probably lend increased credibility to the claims of search activists. As Erica Haimes (135) observed regarding the British debate over the social control of genealogical knowledge in the case of assisted reproduction, the anonymity argument has been taken as a starting point. This is true of gamete donation in the United States as well. But as in the case of adoption, "the sheer fact of wanting to preserve elaborate devices for retaining anonymity [in the case of assisted reproduction] is an indication that the genetic tie is actually regarded as very important indeed" (136).

THE NEED TO KNOW: AN INTERACTIONIST APPROACH

Although search activists have not completely overlooked the social aspects of parenting and identity (e.g., Lifton 1988, 262), they have glossed over the profound social and emotional relationship that is formed in adoption. Instead they have emphasized the biological determinants of feelings of kinship and characterized the need to search as a genetic and universal biological imperative. To searchers, it matters little that the adoptive parents have been allowed the right "to be regarded by the child and society as the real parents" (285), while in the same breath adoptive mothers have been described as "barren wombs." Occasional references to the importance of choice in the search literature mean little if the lack of a desire to search is interpreted as a symptom of negative character traits or individual pathology.

From the writings of search activists, we know enough about adoptees' experiences to conclude that the traditional assumption among adoption experts that early placement and successful matching (see, e.g., Bernard 1963) can secure an unproblematic identity development is flawed. It is also misleading to use the adoptee's adjustment to social demands as an overall measure of identity. According to Leslie M. Stein and Janet L. Hoopes (1985, 4), the primary sign of an adoptee's "consolidated identity" is "the individual's adaptation . . . to the demands of the prevailing role structure of the society in which he or she lives." As with any adjustment to social expectations, there is no guarantee that what is taken as evidence of successful identity development is not really a repression of desires.

On the other hand, Florence Fisher's (1993) comment with regard to the custody battle over "Baby Jessica" that "chromosomes" are the defining elements of a child's "true identity" does not leave much room for a interactionist view of identity and the self. In order to bring the social and cultural context back into adoption research, the experiences of being adopted in a culture that defines adoptive kinship as inferior must be accounted for as well. In contrast to the psychopathological approach employed by most researchers, an interactionist approach along the path staked out by George Herbert Mead recognizes and takes seriously the fact that adoption has traditionally been associated with disparaging attitudes (Triseliotis 1991, 35–44). Although no studies have systematically explored the impact of stigmatizing attitudes and adoptees' sense of self, research indicates that young adoptees in particular are vulnerable to feeling "different" or "bad" because of denigrating comments of their peers (Rosenberg and Horner 1991, 72). In her autobiography, *Nobody's Child*, Marie Balter (Balter and Katz 1991, 4) offers a touching account of the adoption stigma:

> My life really begins in Gloucester, Massachusetts, when I was five years old. Ma and Pa have just adopted me and changed my name to Marie. One hot summer day shortly after I've come to live with Ma and Pa, I hear the shrill, sing-song shouts of the neighbor's children: "We know who you are . . . we know who you are! You don't have a mother! You're adopted." Angry and frustrated, I run to Ruth, a friend of Ma's. Tears fill my eyes and stream down, wetting my cheeks.
>
> "Why are you crying?" Ruth asks.
>
> "The kids . . . the kids say I'm adopted," the words barely escape through my sobs.
>
> As she gently wipes my face, Ruth asks me what I think "adopted" means. All I can say is, "I don't know but it's awful bad!"
>
> Age five, I feel unloved. I feel that I belong to no one and deserve the hatred and contempt of others.

As Erving Goffman (1963, 32) observed in his classic work on stigma, through socialization the stigmatized person learns "the standpoint of the normal, acquiring thereby the identity beliefs of the wider society and a general idea of what it would be like to possess a particular stigma." Emotions cannot be understood apart from the social relations, forms of speech, and frameworks of meaning within which they are experienced and communicated (Franks and McCarthy 1989, xii). Historical studies of the Western family have found that parents' emotional responses have been crucially influenced by the social context of parenting (Shorter 1975), and we have no reason to expect adoptive parents to be an exception. If anything, we should be surprised that so many close adoptive bonds have been formed in spite of disparaging social attitudes.

Recent accounts of gender differences in response to infertility have pointed to important social factors that affect the mental health of infertile couples, such as fertility norms and norms of femininity and masculinity (Abbey, Andrews, and Halman 1992; Greil, Leitko, and Porter 1988; Greil, Porter, and Riscilli 1989; Miall 1986). These researchers have noted the strong impact of stigmatizing attitudes toward childlessness and the different effects of social expectations on men and women. Adoptive parenthood has been shown to be a particularly discrediting social attribute for women, and it is therefore not surprising that some adoptive mothers experience adoption as a second-rate option. A few adoptive mothers continue to attempt to become biological mothers through in vitro fertilization (Williams 1990), and a small minority undergo experimental hormone treatments to be able to breast-feed their adopted babies (*CNN Health Week* 1991).

In her seminal study of the stigma of adoptive parenthood, Charlene Miall (1987) found that two-thirds of the adoptive mothers she interviewed were disturbed by the dominant societal belief that adoptive motherhood is inferior. Many adopters experience the adoption process as problematic, intrusive, and humiliating (Modell 1994, 95). As Kerry Daly (1989) found in her interviews with infertile couples who were planning to adopt, their feelings of anger over their infertility were magnified and reinforced by their powerlessness in the adoption system and the arbitrariness of the adoption process. Their situation was further complicated by the fact that the established "feeling rules" of adoption agencies make it impossible for them to express this anger, since negative emotions tend to be interpreted as signs of individual pathology that make them unsuitable to adopt.

Yet, as I noted in chapter 3, these findings have so far had scant impact on studies of adoption and mental health. Instead, the often-tacit assumption that the adoptive mothers' psychological adjustment is negatively influenced by her inability to bear children has continued to influence adoption research. Although a psychoanalytic or family-systems approach to adoption can be very helpful in terms of individual therapy, it is restrictive as a political strategy. In order to improve the legal rights and social standing of adoptees, birth parents, and adoptive parents, adoption experts as well as search activists must move away from the idealization of certain forms of parenting and consider the possible multitude of families and forms of parenting, including the roles and responsibilities of fathers.

Toward Greater Openness in Adoption

Legal experts have suggested various policy alternatives for resolving the sealed records debate, but the search movement maintains that adoptees should have the *unconditional* right to receive identifying information about their biological parents. Indeed, why should adoptees have to suffer from society's ambivalence regarding the importance of biological and social bonds? Why should adoptees' "compelling needs" be determined by others? The choice to search or not to search must ultimately reside with the adult adoptee, who had no say in the original adoption agreement. Although it is mainly a matter of granting the adoptee's interests paramount legal status, it should also be recalled that we have no reliable information about how many birth and adoptive parents have actually been promised privacy by the adoption agencies and that surveys of both birth and adoptive parents have found them quite receptive to opening adoption records (see chap. 2). In *Family Bonds: Adoption and the Politics of Parenting,* Elizabeth Bartholet (1993, 61) predicts that unlocking adoption files would probably show that the search movement has overemphasized the importance of blood ties. She may be right, and, given their close relationship to their children, adoptive parents may sense this. Although mutual-consent registries should be free of cost to adoptees *and* their biological parents nationwide, adoptees who, through this process, cannot get the information they seek should then, through recourse to the courts, receive all available information, without obstacles. There should be clearer guidelines for state courts: mere curiosity should suffice as a reason to open the records. As I noted in chapter 2, the traditional legal distinction between "mere curiosity" and "compelling need" used in sealed records cases is logically flawed and arbitrary. Clear, legal, nationwide standards are needed. Although psychological counseling should be available to adoptees and their families, it should not be used as a mandatory gatekeeping mechanism, especially not within the dominant psychopathological paradigm (see chap. 3).

Since the 1960s, experts have played a central role in court decisions involving mental health issues, and this procedure has been used in sealed records cases as well. As the history of adoption practice in the United States reveals, however, the knot of knowledge and power cannot be untangled, and the close affinity between expert knowledge and partisan interests is reason for caution. Rather than simply substituting one set of expert opinions for another, we need to make explicit the implicit value assumptions that shape research on adoption. We must ask whether it is really possible to construct a new universal psychology of the adopted based on the experience of some American adoptees as interpreted through the lens of one traditional theory of the self. Like any other field of expertise, the American brand of ego psychology that has been used by the search movement reflects cultural biases and preferences, such as an overemphasis on independence, self-direction, and individualistic explanations (Kirschner 1990). Although there is much to be learned from this tradition of inquiry, individualistic explanations do not suffice—especially not when we are trying to comprehend the mental health needs of stigmatized individuals whose experiences are particularly affected by social norms.

Fairness in the adoption system cannot be achieved by pathologizing adoption and denigrating adoptive bonds. To argue convincingly for the unlocking of court and agency records, it is not necessary to agree with all arguments of the search movement. The realization that the "need to know" has an interactional component that is tied to the social meaning and cultural images of adoption does not in any way detract from the *reality* of this desire. Although the need for self-narratives is as much social as it is innate (Gergen and Gergen 1983), this does not take away from its reality. An interactionist perspective on identity development does not diminish the urgency of the need to know; it only allows for more flexibility and diversity in defining its sources. Arguments based on the *real desire* of adoptees to know or meet their biological relatives need not be based on essentialist or universalist assumptions of innate sources. Considering the weight attributed to the biological underpinnings of parent-child relationships in this society, it is both cruel and unreasonable to expect adoptees and their biological parents to feel otherwise.

Although arguments concerning the biological origins of the need to know remain speculative, we can be sure that in this society knowledge about genetic heritage is generally regarded and experienced as an important part of a person's identity, perhaps even as an archetypal yearning. The burden of proof should therefore be assigned not to adoptees but to the adoption system and its agencies. Since ours is a society that stresses the paramount significance of the blood relation and since adoption professionals in their everyday practices may implicitly reinforce this assumption, the sealed records policy simply demands the impossible from those it affects. Herein lies the most compelling and politically powerful critique of the sealed records policy.

Is there a way to argue for adoption reform without simultaneously perpetuating harmful and confining images of those most intimately affected by adoption? My study would indicate that the possibility of escaping the trappings of rhetoric is slim. Yet I have also attempted to uncover the underlying images and structures of representation that have shaped the debate. There is no way to fully escape the rhetorical imperative, but new insights can replace old ones. In order to move toward openness, however, all parties must make a sincere attempt to recognize one another's needs and viewpoints—"to discover where they are coming from—in personal and institutional terms, including especially the action frames that shape their interests" (Schön and Rein 1994, 207). As Rothman (1989) has argued, the search debate will have to move beyond the preoccupation with biological and genetic imperatives, focus on the experience and social context of child rearing and childbearing and, in the process, acknowledge that both pregnancy and parenting are important and that parenthood, in the true sense, can be determined by either. We must also acknowledge that individuals are capable of not one but many significant attachments and that identities and selves are fashioned through processes so complex that they cannot be adequately explained by means of a single theoretical framework.

References

Abbey, A., Andrews, F. M., and Halman, J. L. (1992). "Infertility and Subjective Well-Being: The Mediating Roles of Self-Esteem, Internal Control, and Interpersonal Conflict." *Journal of Marriage and the Family 54*, 408–17.

Abbott, E. (1937). *Some Pioneers in Social Welfare.* Chicago: University of Chicago Press.

Abercrombie, N., Hill, S., and Turner, B. S. (1980). *The Dominant Ideology Thesis.* London: George Allen and Unwin.

Abernathy, A. (1981). "An Adoptee's Right to Know." University of Missouri at Columbia Freedom of Information Center, Report 441, July.

Adoptees-in-Search (1992). *Why Search?* Bethesda: Adoptees-in-Search.

Adoptees' Liberty Movement Association (1988). *The ALMA Searchlight*, Autumn.

——— (1990). *ALMA San Francisco Bay Area Newsletter 10*, July (no. 2).

Aigner, H. (1986). *Adoption in America Coming of Age.* Greenbrae, Calif.: Paradigm Press.

Alcoff, L., and Grey, L. (1993). "Survivor Discourse: Transgression or Recuperation?" *Signs 18*, 260–90.

Amadio, C. M. (1991). "Doing the Right Thing: Some Ethical Considerations in Current Adoption Practice." *Social Thought 17*, 25–33.

Amadio, C. M., and Deutsch, S. L. (1983–84). "Open Adoption: Allowing Adopted Children to 'Stay in Touch' with Blood Relatives." *Journal of Family Law 22*, 59–93.

Andersen, M. L. (1991). "Feminism and the American Family Ideal." *Journal of Comparative Family Studies 22*, 235–46.

Andersen, R. S. (1988). "Why Adoptees Search: Motives and More." *Child Welfare 67*, 15–19.

√Arms, S. (1990). *Adoption: A Handful of Hope.* Berkeley: Celestial Arts. Originally published as *To Love and Let Go*, New York: Knopf, 1983.

√Arndt, M. (1986). "Severed Roots: The Sealed Adoption Records Controversy." *Northern Illinois University Law Review 6*, 103–27.

Aumend, S. A., and Barrett, M. C. (1984). "Self-Concept and Attitudes toward Adoption: A Comparison of Searching and Nonsearching Adult Adoptees." *Child Welfare 63*, 251–59.

Austin, D. M. (1983). "The Flexner Myth and the History of Social Work." *Social Service Review 57*, 357–77.

Auth, P. J., and Zaret, S. (1986). "The Search in Adoption: A Service and a Process." *Social Casework 67*, 560–68.

Bachrach, C., Adams, P. F., Samrano, S., and London, K. A. (1990). "Adoption in the 1980s." *Advance Data from Vital Health Statistics 18*, 1–12.

Bailey, M. D. (1957). *Maxwell Anderson: The Playwright as Prophet*. London: Abelard-Schuman.

Balter, M., and Katz, R. (1991). *Nobody's Child*. Reading: Addison-Wesley.

Baran, A., Pannor, R., and Sorosky, A. D. (1976). "Open Adoption." *Social Work 21*, 97–100.

Barthes, R. (1977). *Image, Music, Text*. New York: Farrar, Straus and Giroux.

Bartholet, E. (1993). *Family Bonds: Adoption and the Politics of Parenting*. Boston: Houghton Mifflin.

Beckman, G. M. (1985). "Changes Highlight Need for Making Special Provisions for Adopted or Illegitimate Children." *Estate Planning 12*, 352–55.

Benet, M. K. (1976). *The Politics of Adoption*. New York: Free Press.

Benford, R. D., and Hunt, S. A. (1992). "Dramaturgy and Social Movements: The Social Construction and Communication of Power." *Sociological Inquiry 61*, 36–55.

Benson, P. L., Sharma, A., and Roehlkepartain, E. C. (1994). *Growing Up Adopted: A Portrait of Adolescents and Their Families*. Minneapolis: The Search Institute.

Bernard, V. W. (1963). "Adoption." In A. Deutsch and H. Fishman (eds.), *Encyclopedia of Mental Health*, vol. 1, pp. 70–108. New York: Franklin Watts.

Bernardes, J. (1985). "'Family Ideology': Identification and Exploration." *Sociological Review 33*, 275–97.

Berry, M. (1992). "Contributors to Adjustment Problems of Adoptees: A Review of the Longitudinal Research." *Child and Adolescent Social Work 9*, 525–40.

Bertocci, D., and Schechter, M. D. (1991). "Adopted Adults' Perception of Their Need to Search: Implications for Clinical Practice." *Smith College Studies in Social Work 61,* 179–96.

Best, J. (1987). "Dark Figures and Child Victims: Statistical Claims about Missing Children." In J. Best (ed.), *Images of Issues: Typifying Social Problems,* pp. 21–37. New York: Aldine de Gruyter.

Bettelheim, B. (1985). *Freud and Man's Soul.* London: Fontana.

Billig, M., Condor, S., Edwards, D., Gane, M., Middleton, D., and Radley, A. (1988). *Ideological Dilemmas: A Social Psychology of Everyday Thinking.* London: Sage.

"Blood Is Thicker Than Surnames: Reunion of Adopted Triplets" (1988). *Newsweek,* October 6, 61.

Bolen, J. S. (1993). *Ring of Power: The Abandoned Child, the Authoritarian Father, and the Disempowered Feminine.* San Francisco: HarperCollins.

Boswell, J. (1988). *The Kindness of Strangers: The Abandonment of Children in Western Europe from Late Antiquity to the Renaissance.* New York: Pantheon.

Bowen, J. S. (1987/1988). "Cultural Convergences and Divergences: The Nexus between Putative Afro-American Family Values and the Best Interests of the Child." *Journal of Family Law 26,* 487–532.

Brinich, P. M., and Brinich, E. B. (1982). "Adoption and Adaptation." *Journal of Nervous and Mental Disease 170,* 489–97.

Brodzinsky, A. (1990). "Surrendering an Infant for Adoption: The Birthmother Experience." In D. M. Brodzinsky and M. D. Schechter (eds.), ✳ *The Psychology of Adoption,* pp. 295–315. New York: Oxford University Press.

Brodzinsky, D. M. (1990). "The Stress and Coping Model of Adoption." In D. M. Brodzinsky and M. D. Schechter (eds.), *The Psychology of Adoption,* pp. 3–24. New York: Oxford University Press.

——— (1993). "Long-Term Outcomes in Adoption." *The Future of Children 3,* 153–66.

Burgess, L. C. (1981). *The Art of Adoption.* New York: Norton.

Burke, K. (1957). *The Philosophy of Literary Form.* New York: Vintage Books.

Burton, T. (director) (1992). *Batman Returns.* Warner Brothers.

Byrd, A. D. (1988). "The Case for Confidential Adoption." *Public Welfare 46,* 20–23.

Cadoret, R. J. (1990). "Biologic Perspectives on Adoptee Adjustment." In D. M. Brodzinsky and M. D. Schechter (eds.), *The Psychology of Adoption,* pp. 25–41. New York: Oxford University Press.

Campbell, L. H., Silverman, P. R., and Patti, P. B. (1991). "Reunions between Adoptees and Birth Parents: The Adoptees' Experience." *Social Work 36*, 329–35.

Caplan, L. (1990). *An Open Adoption.* New York: Farrar, Straus and Giroux.

Caplan, P. J. (1985). *Don't Blame the Mother: Mending the Mother-Daughter Relationship.* New York: Harper and Row.

Carbaugh, D. (1989). *Talking American: Cultural Discourses on Donahue.* Norwood: Ablex.

Carby, H. V. (1992). "Policing the Black Woman's Body in an Urban Context." *Critical Inquiry 18*, 738–55.

Carlson, P. M. (1991). *Bad Blood.* New York: Doubleday.

Carp, E. W. (1992). "The Sealed Records Controversy in Historical Perspective: The Case of the Children's Home Society of Washington, 1895–1988." *Journal of Sociology and Social Welfare 19*, 27–57.

Cashman, F. (1979). "Origins: New Challenges for Adoption Agencies." *Social Thought 5*, 15–23.

Cathcart, R. (1980). "Movements: Confrontation as Rhetorical Form." In R. L. Scott and B. L. Brock (eds.), *Methods of Rhetorical Criticism*, pp. 436–57. Detroit: Wayne State University Press.

✱ Chambers, D. E. (1975). "The Adoption of Strangers." *International Journal of Comparative Sociology 16*, 118–25.

Chapman, B. (1989). "Adoption Is an Orphan." *Washington Post,* April 21, A27.

Chesler, P. (1989). *The Sacred Bond: The Legacy of Baby M.* New York: Vintage.

Chimezie, A. (1975). "Transracial Adoption of Black Children." *Social Work 20*, 296–301.

Churchman, D. (1986). "The Debate over Open Adoption." *Public Welfare 44*, 11–14.

CNN Health Week (1991). "Mother's Milk." Cable News Network. April 27, transcript 63.

Cohen, J. L. (1985). "Strategy or Identity: New Theoretical Paradigms and Contemporary Social Movements." *Social Research 52*, 663–716.

✱ Cole, E., and Donley, K. S. (1990). "History, Values and Placement Issues in Adoption." In D. M. Brodzinsky and M. D. Schechter (eds.), *The Psychology of Adoption*, pp. 237–94. New York: Oxford University Press.

Cominos, H. (1971). "Minimizing the Risk of Adoption through Knowledge." *Social Work 16*, 73–79.

Comment (1993). "Adoption Country." *New Yorker,* May 10, 6–7.

Condit, C. M. (1990). *Decoding Abortion Rhetoric: Communicating Social Change*. Urbana: University of Illinois Press.

Coser, L. A. (1963). *Sociology Through Literature*. Englewood Cliffs: Prentice-Hall.

Crane, A. E. (1986). "Unsealing Adoption Records: The Right to Know versus the Right to Privacy." *Annual Survey of American Law 2*, 645–66.

Curtis, P. A. (1990). "An Ethnographic Study of Pregnancy Counseling." *Clinical Social Work Journal 18*, 243–56.

Daly, K. J. (1989). "Anger among Prospective Adoptive Parents: Structural Determinants and Management Strategies." *Clinical Sociology Review 7*, 80–96.

———— (1990). "Infertility Resolution and Adoption Readiness." *Families in Society 71*, 483–92.

Davis, K. (1939–40). "Illegitimacy and the Social Structure." *American Journal of Sociology 45*, 215–33.

Dean, A. (1991). *Letters to My Birthmother*. New York: Pharos.

Deutsch, H. (1945). *The Psychology of Women*. Vol. 2. New York: Grune and Stratton.

DeWoody, M. (1993). "Adoption and the Disclosure of Medical and Social History: A Review of the Law." *Child Welfare 72*, 195–218.

✳ DiGiulio, J. F. (1988). "Self-Acceptance: A Factor in the Adoption Process." *Child Welfare 117*, 423–29.

Dingwall, R., Eekelaar, J., and Murray, T. (1983). *The Protection of Children: State Intervention and Family Life*. Oxford: Blackwell.

Donahue (1986). Central Broadcasting System. November 17, transcript 11176.

———— (1989). "Birth Moms Reluctantly Reunited with the Children They Gave Away." Central Broadcasting System. March 16, transcript 2643.

———— (1991). Central Broadcasting System. November 6, transcript 11061.

Donzelot, J. (1978). *The Policing of Families*. Translated by R. Hurley. New York: Pantheon.

Dressel, P. (1987). "Patriarchy and Social Welfare Work." *Social Problems 34*, 294–309.

Dukette, R. (1984). "Value Issues in Present-Day Adoption." *Child Welfare 63*, 223–43.

Dusky, L. (1979). *Birthmark*. New York: M. Evans.

Eagleton, T. (1991). *Ideology: An Introduction*. London: Verso.

Eisenstein, Z. R. (1988). *The Female Body and the Law*. Berkeley: University of California Press.

Elliot, F. R. (1986). "The Family: Private Arena or Adjunct of the State?" *Journal of Law and Society 16*, 443–63.

Emery, J. L. (1993). "Agency versus Independent Adoption: The Case for Agency Adoption." *The Future of Children 3*, 139–52.

Erikson, K. T. (1976). *Everything in Its Path: Destruction of Community in the Buffalo Creek Flood*. New York: Simon and Schuster.

Eyer, D. E. (1992). *Mother-Infant Bonding: A Scientific Fiction*. New Haven: Yale University Press.

Fay, J. J. (1987). "The Mutual Consent Voluntary Adoption Registry: A Sound Approach to the Sealed Records Controversy." *Rutgers Law Journal 18*, 663–85.

Feigelman, W., and Silverman, A. R. (1983). <u>*Chosen Children: New Patterns of Adoptive Kinship.*</u> New York: Praeger.

———— (1986). "Adoptive Parents, Adoptees, and the Sealed Records Controversy." *Social Case Work* (April), 219–26.

Felski, R. (1989). "Feminist Theory and Social Change." *Theory, Culture and Society 6*, 219–40.

Fieweger, M. E. (1991). "Stolen Children and International Adoptions." *Child Welfare 70*, 285–91.

Fish, S. (1989). *Doing What Comes Naturally: Change, Rhetoric, and the Practice of Theory in Literary and Legal Studies*. Durham: Duke University Press.

Fisher, F. (1973). *The Search for Anna Fisher*. New York: Arthur Field.

———— (1988). "President's Message: State Registries — Solution or Sabotage?" *The ALMA Searchlight*, Autumn.

———— (1993). "Adopted Child's Heredity Is Not a Blank Slate" (Letter to the Editor). *New York Times*, May 9.

Flango, V. E. (1990). "Agency and Private Adoptions, by State." *Child Welfare 69*, 263–75.

Foster, A. (1979). "Who Has the 'Right' to Know?" *Public Welfare 37*, 34–37.

Foucault, M. (1978). *The History of Sexuality*. Vol. 1, *An Introduction*. Translated by R. Hurley. New York: Pantheon.

———— (1980). "Two Lectures." In C. Gordon (ed.), *Power/Knowledge: Selected Interviews and Other Writings 1972–1977*, pp. 78–108. New York: Pantheon.

Fox, W. F., Jr. (1979). "Anonymity in the Adoption Process: The Legal Aspects." *Social Thought 5*, 43–52.

Francke, L. B. (1975). "Adoptees Unite." *Newsweek,* April 28, 86.

Franklin, D. L. (1986). "Mary Richmond and Jane Addams: From Moral Certainty to Rational Inquiry in Social Work Practice." *Social Service Review 60,* 504–25.

Franks, D. D., and McCarthy, E. D. (1989). "Introduction." In D. D. Franks and E. D. McCarthy (eds.), *The Sociology of Emotions: Original Essays and Research Papers,* pp. xi–xx. Greenwich, Conn.: JAI Press.

Freedman, D. H. (1979). *Human Sociobiology: A Holistic Approach.* New York: Free Press.

Freidson, E. (1970). *The Profession of Medicine: A Study of the Sociology of Applied Knowledge.* Chicago: University of Chicago Press.

Gamson, J. (1995). "Identity Movements (review essay)." *Contemporary Sociology 24,* 294–98.

Gamson, W. A., Croteau, D., Hoynes, W., and Sasson, T. (1992). "Media Images and the Social Construction of Reality." *Annual Review of Sociology 18,* 384–93.

Gamson, W. A., and Modigliani, A. (1989). "Media Discourse and Public Opinion on Nuclear Power: A Constructionist Approach." *American Journal of Sociology 95,* 1–37.

Gamson, W. A., and Stuart, D. (1992). "Media Discourse as Symbolic Contest: The Bomb in Political Cartoons." *Sociological Forum 7,* 55–86.

Geraldo (1988a). "Eliminating the Pain of Adoption." American Broadcasting Company. July 28, transcript 225.

——— (1988b). "Private Adoption: White Knights or Flesh Peddlers?" American Broadcasting Company. December 1, transcript 316.

——— (1991a). "Reunions of the Heart: Finding a Long Lost Love." American Broadcasting Company. July 26, transcript 1007.

——— (1991b). "Illegitimate Kids Who Found Their Parents . . . but Wish They Hadn't." American Broadcasting Company. September 18, transcript 1045.

Gerbner, G. (1988). Adoption in the Mass Media. Annenberg School of Communications, University of Pennsylvania, typescript.

Gergen, K. J., and Gergen, M. M. (1983). "Narratives of the Self." In T. R. Sarbin and K. E. Scheibe (eds.), *Studies in Social Identity,* pp. 254–73. New York: Praeger.

Gesell, A. (1927). "Reducing the Risks of Child Adoption." *Child Welfare League of America Bulletin 6,* 1–2.

Gibbs, N. (1989). "The Baby Chase." *Time,* October 9, 86–89.

Giddens, A. (1984). *The Constitution of Society.* Berkeley: University of California Press.

———— (1990). *The Consequences of Modernity*. Stanford: Stanford University Press.

———— (1991). *Modernity and Self-Identity: Self and Society in the Late Modern Age*. Stanford: Stanford University Press.

Gilligan, C. (1982). *In a Different Voice: Psychological Theory and Women's Development*. Cambridge: Harvard University Press.

Gilmore, L. (1994). *Autobiographics: A Feminist Theory of Women's Self-Representation*. Ithaca: Cornell University Press.

Ginsburg, F. D. (1989). *Contested Lives: The Abortion Debate in an American Community*. Berkeley: University of California Press.

Gitlin, T. (1979). "Prime Time Ideology: The Hegemonic Process in Television Entertainment." *Social Problems 26*, 251–66.

Glenn, E. N. (1994). "Social Constructions of Mothering: A Thematic Overview." In E. N. Glenn, G. Chang, and L. R. Forcey (eds.), *Mothering: Ideology, Experience, and Agency*, pp. 1–29. New York: Routledge.

Glenn, J. (1974). "The Adoption Theme in Edward Albee's *Tiny Alice* and *The American Dream*." *Psychoanalytic Study of the Child 29*, 413–24.

Glenn, N. D. (1991). "A Conjugal Study of Kin Relations outside the Nuclear Family" (review essay). *Contemporary Sociology 20*, 669–71.

Goffman, E. (1963). *Stigma: Notes on the Management of Spoiled Identity*. Englewood Cliffs: Prentice-Hall.

Goldstein, H. (1990). "The Knowledge Base of Social Work Practice: Theory, Wisdom, Analogue or Art?" *Families in Society 71*, 32–43.

Goldstein, J., Freud, A., and Solnit, A. J. (1973). *Beyond the Best Interests of the Child*. New York: Free Press.

Gonyo, B., and Watson, K. D. (1979). "Searching in Adoption." *Public Welfare 37*, 4–22.

———— (1988). "Searching in Adoption." *Public Welfare 46*, 14–22.

Goody, J. (1969). "Adoption in Cross-cultural Perspective." *Comparative Studies in Society and History 11*, 55–78.

Gordon, L. (1985). "Single Mothers and Child Neglect, 1880–1940." *American Quarterly 37*, 173–92.

Greil, A. L., Leitko, T. A., and Porter, K. A. (1988). "Infertility: His and Hers." *Gender and Society 2*, 17.–99.

Greil, A. L., Porter, T. A., and Riscilli, C. (1989). "Why Me? Theodicies of Infertile Women and Men." *Sociology of Health and Illness 11*, 213–29.

Griffin, C. J. G. (1990). "The Rhetoric of Form in Conversion Narratives." *Quarterly Journal of Speech 76*, 152–63.

Gusdorf, G. (1980). "Conditions and Limits of Autobiography." In

J. Olney (ed.), *Autobiography: Essays Theoretical and Critical*, pp. 28-48. Princeton: Princeton University Press.

Gusfield, J. R. (1963). *Symbolic Crusade: Status Politics and the American Temperance Movement*. Urbana: University of Illinois Press.

―― (1981). *The Culture of Public Problems: Drinking-Driving and the Symbolic Order*. Chicago: University of Chicago Press.

―― (1989). "Introduction." In J. R. Gusfield (ed.), *Kenneth Burke: On Symbols and Society*, pp. 1-49. Chicago: University of Chicago Press.

―― (1994). "Reflexivity of Social Movements: Collective Behavior and Mass Theory Revisited." In E. Laraña, H. Johnston, and J. R. Gusfield (eds.), *New Social Movements: From Ideology to Identity*, pp. 58-78. Philadelphia: Temple University Press.

Habermas, J. (1972). *Knowledge and Human Interests*. Translated by J. J. Shapiro. Boston: Beacon Press.

―― (1981). "New Social Movements." *Telos*, no. 49, 33-37.

Hahn, D. F., and Gonchar, R. M. (1971). "Studying Social Movements: A Rhetorical Methodology." *Speech Teacher 20*, 44-52.

Haimes, E. (1992). "Gamete Donation and the Social Management of Genetic Origins." In M. Stacey (ed.), *Changing Human Reproduction: Social Science Perspective*, pp. 119-49. London: Sage.

Haimes, E., and Timms, N. (1985). *Adoption, Identity and Social Policy: The Search for Distant Relatives*. Aldershot: Gower.

Hajal, F., and Rosenberg, E. B. (1991). "The Family Life Cycle in Adoptive Families." *American Journal of Orthopsychiatry 61*, 78-85.

Hamilton, R. (1990). "Feminism and Motherhood, 1970-1990: Reinventing the Wheel?" *Resources for Feminist Research 19*, 23-32.

Hayes, P. (1993). "Transracial Adoption: Politics and Ideology." *Child Welfare 72*, 301-10.

Herrman, K. J., and Kasper, B. (1992). "International Adoption: The Exploitation of Women and Children." *Affilia 7*, 45-58.

Hicks, B. (1995). "Who Cares Who My Birth Parents Are?" *Parade Magazine*, March 12, 31.

Hilgartner, S., and Bosk, C. L. (1988). "The Rise and Fall of Social Problems: A Public Arenas Model." *American Journal of Sociology 94*, 53-78.

Hirschman, A. O. (1991). *The Rhetoric of Reaction: Perversity, Futility, Jeopardy*. Cambridge: Harvard University Press.

Hoffmann-Riem, C. (1990). *The Adopted Child: Family Life with Double Parenthood*. New Brunswick: Transaction.

Hollinger, J. H. (1993). "Adoption Law." *The Future of Children 3*, 43–61.

Hoopes, J. L. (1985). *Identity Formation in the Adopted Adolescent.* New York: Child Welfare League of America.

Horn, J. M. (1983). "The Texas Adoption Project: Adopted Children and Their Intellectual Resemblance to Biological and Adoptive Parents." *Child Development 54*, 268–75.

Houlgate, L. D. (1988). *Family and State: The Philosophy of Family Law.* Totowa: Rowman and Littlefield.

Howard, M. D. (1990). "The Adoptee's Dilemma: Obstacles in Identity Formation." In P. V. Grabe (ed.), *Adoption Resources for Mental Health Professionals*, pp. 243–58. New Brunswick: Transaction.

Howe, R. A. W. (1983). "Adoption Practice, Issues, and Law: 1958–1983." *Family Law Quarterly 17*, 173–97.

Hubbard, R. (1982). "Have Only Men Evolved?" In R. Hubbard, M. S. Henifin, and B. Fried (eds.). *Biological Woman: The Convenient Myth*, pp. 17–45. Cambridge: Schenkman.

Hudgens, L. D. (1980). "I Gave My Daughter Away—and Found Her Again." *Ladies' Home Journal*, March, 23–24.

Humphrey, M., and Humphrey, H. (1980). *Families with a Difference: Varieties of Surrogate Parenthood.* London: Routledge.

Hutchby, I. (1992). "The Pursuit of Controversy: Routine Skepticism in Talk on 'Talk Radio.'" *Sociology 26*, 673–94.

James, P. D. (1982). *Innocent Blood.* New York: Warner.

Johnson, J. M. (1989). "Horror Stories and the Construction of Child Abuse." In J. Best (ed.), *Images of Issues: Typifying Contemporary Social Problems*, pp. 5–19. New York: Aldine de Gruyter.

Johnson, T. (1992). "Governmentality and the Institutionalization of Expertise." Paper presented at symposium, *Professions in Transition.* International Sociological Association, University of Leicester, England, April 21–23.

Johnston, H., Laraña, E., and Gusfield, J. R. (1994). "Identities, Grievances, and the New Social Movements." In E. Laraña, H. Johnston, and J. R. Gusfield (eds.), *New Social Movements: From Ideology to Identity*, pp. 3–35. Philadelphia: Temple University Press.

Jones, M. A. (1976). *The Sealed Adoption Records Controversy: Report of a Survey of Agency Policy, Practice and Opinions.* New York: Child Welfare League of America.

Journal Graphics (1994). *Topic Alert Hits, April 1993–March 1994.* Denver: Journal Graphics.

Kadushin, A. (1966). "Adoptive Parenthood: A Hazardous Adventure?" *Social Work 11*, 30–39.

Kadushin, A., and Martin, J. A. (1988). *Child Welfare Services*, 4th ed. New York: Macmillan.

Kawashima, Y. (1981–82). "Adoption in Early America." *Family Law Quarterly 20*, 677–96.

"Keep Adoption a Secret" (1960). *Science Newsletter*, July 23, 52.

Kirk, H. D. (1964). *Shared Fate: A Theory of Adoption and Mental Health*. New York: Free Press.

——— (1985). *Adoptive Kinship: A Modern Institution in Need of Reform*. Port Angeles, Wash.: Ben-Simon.

Kirk, H. D., Jonassohn, K., and Fish, A. D. (1966). "Are Adopted Children Especially Vulnerable to Stress?" *Archives of General Psychiatry 14*, 291–98.

Kirk, H. D., and McDaniel, S. A. (1984). "Adoption in Great Britain and North America." *Journal of Social Policy 13*, 75–84.

Kirschner, D. H. (1992). "Understanding Adoptees Who Kill: Dissociation, Patricide, and the Psychodynamics of Adoption." *International Journal of Offender Therapy and Comparative Criminology 36*, 323–33.

Kirschner, D. H., and Nagel, L. S. (1988). "Antisocial Behavior in Adoptees: Patterns and Dynamics." *Child and Adolescent Social Work 5*, 300–14.

Kirschner, S. R. (1990). "The Assenting Echo: Anglo-American Values in Contemporary Psychoanalytic Developmental Psychology." *Social Research 57*, 821–57.

Kowal, K. A., and Shilling, K. M. (1985). "Adoption through the Eyes of Adult Adoptees." *American Journal of Orthopsychiatry 55*, 354–62.

Kraft, A. D., Palombo, J., Woods, P. K., Mitchell, D., and Schmidt, A. W. (1985). "Some Theoretical Considerations on Confidential Adoptions." Pt. 1, "The Birth Mother." *Child and Adolescent Social Work 2*, 13–21.

Kunzel, R. G. (1993). *Fallen Women, Problem Girls: Unmarried Women and the Professionalization of Social Work, 1890–1945*. New Haven: Yale University Press.

Lakoff, G., and Johnson, M. (1980). *Metaphors We Live By*. Chicago: University of Chicago Press.

Larson, M. S. (1977). *The Rise of Professionalism: A Sociological Analysis*. Berkeley: University of California Press.

Lauritzen, P. (1993). *Pursuing Parenthood: Ethical Issues in Assisted Reproduction*. Bloomington: Indiana University Press.

Lawder, E. A., Lower, K. D., Andrews, R. G., Sherman, E. A., and Hill, J. G. (1969). *A Followup Study of Adoptions: Post-Placement Functioning of Adoptive Families.* New York: Child Welfare League of America.

Lawrence, E. M. (1981). "The State's Interest in Adoption and Washington's Sealed Records Policy." *University of Puget Sound Law Review 4,* 351–84.

Letherby, G. (1994). "Mother or Not, Mother or What? Problems of Definition and Identity." *Women's Studies International Forum 17,* 525–32.

"Letters to the Editor" (1988). *Archives of General Psychiatry 45,* 875–77.

LeVine, E. S., and Sallee, A. L. (1990). "Critical Phases among Adoptees and Their Families: Implications for Therapy." *Child and Adolescent Social Work 7,* 217–32.

Lewis, J. (1991). *The Ideological Octopus: An Exploration of Television and Its Audience.* New York: Routledge.

Lewontin, R., Rose, S., and Kamin, L. (1984). *Not in Our Genes: Biology, Ideology, and Human Behavior.* New York: Pantheon.

Lifton, B. J. (1976). "The Search." *New York Times Magazine,* January 25, 15–19.

——— (1977). *Twice Born: Memoirs of an Adopted Daughter.* 2d ed. New York: Penguin.

——— (1988). *Lost and Found: The Adoption Experience.* New York: Harper and Row.

——— (1994). *Journey of the Adopted Self: A Quest for Wholeness.* New York: Basic.

Litt, A. D. (1971). "Psychological vs. Biological Parenthood in Determining the Best Interests of the Child." *Seton Hall Law Review 3,* 130–42.

Luker, K. (1985). *Abortion and the Politics of Motherhood.* Berkeley: University of California Press.

McAdam, D. (1994). "Culture and Social Movements." In E. Laraña, H. Johnston, and J. R. Gusfield (eds.), *New Social Movements: From Ideology to Identity,* pp. 36–57. Philadelphia: Temple University Press.

McKelvey, C. A., and Stevens, J. (1994). *Adoption Crisis: The Truth behind Adoption and Foster Care.* Golden, Colo.: Fulcrum.

McLeod, J. R. (1990). "Deconstructing Bush: Political Rhetoric and the Bush Campaign." *International Journal of Moral and Social Studies 5,* 3–22.

McRoy, R. G., Grotevant, H. D., and Zurcher, L. A., Jr. (1988). *Emo-*

tional Disturbances in Adopted Adolescents: Origins and Development.
New York: Praeger.

Maher, L. (1992). "Punishment and Welfare: Crack Cocaine and the Regulation of Mothering." *Women and Criminal Justice 3,* 15–70.

Mandell, B. R. (1973). *Where Are the Children? A Class Analysis of Foster Care and Adoption.* Lexington, Mass.: Lexington Books.

Manson, P. H. (1979). "Confidentiality of Adoption Records: Can the Real Needs of the Adoptee Be Satisfied?" *Loyola Law Review 25,* 787–98.

Maroney, H. J. (1990). "Embracing Motherhood: New Feminist Theory." *Canadian Journal of Political and Social Theory 9,* 268–82.

Marquis, K. S., and Detweiler, R. A. (1985). "Does Adopted Mean Different? An Attributional Analysis." *Journal of Personality and Social Psychology 48,* 1054–66.

Mason, M. A. (1994). *From Father's Property to Children's Rights: The History of Child Custody in the United States.* New York: Columbia University Press.

Maxtone-Graham, K. (1983). *An Adopted Woman.* New York: Remi.

Mednick, S. A., Gabrielli, W. F., and Hutchings, B. (1984). "Genetic Influences in Criminal Convictions: Evidence from an Adoption Cohort." *Science 224,* 891–94.

Melina, L., and Rozia, S. K. (1993). *The Open Adoption Experience.* New York: Guilford Press.

Menlove, F. L. (1965). "Aggressive Symptoms in Emotionally Disturbed Adopted Children." *Child Development 36,* 519–32.

Merton, R. K. (1976). *Sociological Ambivalence and Other Essays.* New York: Free Press.

Miall, C. (1986). "The Stigma of Involuntary Childlessness." *Social Problems 33,* 268–82.

———— (1987). "The Stigma of Adoptive Parent Status: Perceptions of Community Attitudes toward Adoption and the Experience of Informal Sanctioning." *Family Relations 36,* 34–39.

Mills, C. W. (1940). "Situated Actions and Vocabularies of Motive." *American Sociological Review 5,* 904–13.

Minow, M. (1990). *Making All the Difference: Inclusion, Exclusion, and American Law.* Ithaca: Cornell University Press.

Mishler, E. (1986). *Research Interviewing: Context and Narrative.* Cambridge: Harvard University Press.

Mnookin, R. H. (1985). *In the Best Interest of Children: Advocacy, Law Reform and Public Policy.* New York: Freeman.

Mnookin, R. H., and Weisberg, K. D. (1989). *Child, Family and State: Problems and Materials on Children and the Law*. Boston: Little, Brown.

Modell, J. S. (1986). "In Search: The Purported Biological Basis of Parenthood." *American Ethnologist 13*, 646–61.

——— (1992). "How Do You Introduce Yourself as a Childless Mother?" In G. C. Rosenwald and R. L. Ochberg (eds.), *Storied Lives: The Cultural Politics of Self-Understanding*, pp. 76–94. New Haven: Yale University Press.

——— (1994). *Kinship with Strangers: Adoption and Interpretations of Kinship in American Culture*. Berkeley: University of California Press.

Munson, W. (1993). *All Talk: The Talkshow in Media Culture*. Philadelphia: Temple University Press.

National Committee for Adoption (1989). *1989 Adoption Factbook: United States Data, Issues, Regulations and Resources*. Washington, D.C.: National Committee for Adoption.

National Conference of Commissioners on Uniform State Laws (1994). *Uniform Adoption Act*. Chicago: National Conference of Commissioners on Uniform State Laws.

Nelkin, D., and Lindee, S. M. (1995). *The DNA Mystique: The Gene as a Cultural Icon*. New York: Freeman.

Offe, C. (1985). "New Social Movements: Challenging the Boundaries of Institutional Politics." *Social Research 52*, 817–68.

Offord, D. R., Laponte, J. F., and Cross, L. A. (1969). "Presenting a Symptomatology of Adopted Children." *Archives of General Psychiatry 20*, 110–16.

Ohrenstein, P. (1995). "Looking for a Donor to Call Dad." *New York Times Magazine*, June 18.

Olney, J. (1980). *Autobiography: Essays Theoretical and Critical*. Princeton: Princeton University Press.

Oprah Winfrey Show (1990). "Holiday Reunions for Separated Families." Central Broadcasting System. December 19, transcript 1113.

Pacheco, F., and Eme, R. (1993). "An Outcome Study of the Reunion between Adoptees and Biological Parents." *Child Welfare 72*, 53–64.

Pannor, R., Baran, A. and Sorosky, A. D. (1978). "Birth Parents Who Relinquished Babies for Adoption Revisited." *Family Process 17*, 329–37.

Paton, J. M. (1954). *The Adopted Break Silence: The Experiences and Views of Forty Adults Who Were Adopted as Children*. Philadelphia: Life History Center.

Phoenix, A., and Woollett, A. (1991). "Motherhood: Social Construction, Politics and Psychology." In A. Phoenix, A. Woollett, and E. Lloyd (eds.), *Motherhood: Meanings, Practices and Ideologies*, pp. 13–27. London: Sage.

Pierce, W. (1990). "Family Secret." *CBS News: 48 Hours*. Cable News Network. November 28, transcript 132.

Prager, B., and Rothstein, S. A. (1973). "The Adoptee's Right to Know His Natural Heritage." *New York Law Forum 19*, 137–56.

Presser, S. B. (1971). "The Historical Background of the American Law of Adoption." *Journal of Family Law 11*, 443–516.

Rapping, E. (1987). *The Looking Glass World of Nonfiction TV.* Boston: South End Press.

——— (1990). "The Future of Motherhood: Some Unfashionably Visionary Thoughts." In K. V. Hansen and I. J. Philipson (eds.), *Women, Class, and the Feminist Imagination*, pp. 537–48. Philadelphia: Temple University Press.

Reece, S. A., and Levin, B. (1968). "Psychiatric Disturbances in Adopted Children: A Descriptive Study." *Social Work 13*, 101–11.

Reid, J. H. (1957). "Principles, Values, and Assumptions Underlying Adoption Practice." *Social Work 2*, 22–29.

Reitz, M., and Watson, K. W. (1992). *Adoption and the Family System.* New York: Guilford Press.

Riben, M. (1988). *Shedding Light on the Dark Side of Adoption.* Detroit: Harlo Press.

Rice, J. S. (1992). "Discursive Formation, Life Stories, and the Emergence of Co-dependency: Power/Knowledge and the Search for Identity." *Sociological Quarterly 33*, 337–64.

Riessman, C. K. (1990). *Divorce Talk: Women and Men Make Sense of Personal Relationships.* New Brunswick: Rutgers University Press.

Ripple, L. A. (1968). "A Follow-up Study of Adopted Children." *Social Services Review 42*, 479–99.

Rojek, C., Peacock, G., and Collins, S. (1988). *Social Work and Received Ideas.* London: Routledge.

Rosenberg, E. B., and Horner, T. M. (1991). "Birthparent Romances and Identity Formation in Adopted Children." *American Journal of Orthopsychiatry 61*, 70–77.

Rosenwald, G. C. (1992). "Conclusion: Reflections on Narrative Self-Understanding." In G. C. Rosenwald and R. Ochberg (eds.), *Storied Lives: The Cultural Politics of Self-Understanding*, pp. 265–89. New Haven: Yale University Press.

Rosenwald, G. C., and Ochberg, R. L. (1992). "Introduction: Life Stories, Cultural Politics, and Self-Understanding." In G. C. Rosenwald and R. L. Ochberg (eds.), *Storied Lives: The Cultural Politics of Self-Understanding*, pp. 1-18. New Haven: Yale University Press.

Rothman, B. K. (1989). *Recreating Motherhood: Ideology and Technology in a Patriarchal Society.* New York: Norton.

Rowbothman, S. (1989). "To Be or Not to Be? The Dilemmas of Mothering." *Feminist Review 3,* 81-93.

Sachdev, P. (1989). *Unlocking the Adoption Files.* Lexington, Mass.: Lexington Books.

——— (1991). "The Birth Father: A Neglected Element in the Adoption Equation." *Families in Society 72,* 131-39.

——— (1992). "Adoption Reunion and After: A Study of the Search Process and Experience of Adoptees." *Child Welfare 71,* 53-68.

Sally Jessy Raphael (1991). "I Found My Mother and Hate Her." Central Broadcasting System. June 27, transcript 733.

Schaefer, C. (1992). *The Other Mother: A True Story.* New York: Soho Press.

Schechter, M. D. (1960). "Observations on Adopted Children." *Archives of General Psychiatry 3,* 21-32.

Schechter, M. D., and Bertocci, D. (1990). "The Meaning of the Search." In D. M. Brodzinsky and M. D. Schechter (eds.), *The Psychology of Adoption,* pp. 62-90. New York: Oxford University Press.

Scheibe, K. (1986). "Self-Narrative and Adventure." In T. Sarbin (ed.), *Narrative Psychology,* pp. 129-51. New York: Praeger.

Schneider, D. M. (1980). *American Kinship: A Cultural Account.* Chicago: University of Chicago Press.

Schneider, J. W. (1985). "Social Problems Theory: The Constructionist View." *Annual Review of Sociology 11,* 209-29.

Schneider, S., and Rimmer, E. (1984). "Adoptive Parents' Hostility toward Their Adopted Children." *Children and Youth Services Review 6,* 345-52.

Schön, D. A., and Rein, M. A. (1994). *Frame Reflection: Toward the Resolution of Intractable Policy Controversies.* New York: Basic.

Schulman, I., and Behrman, R. E. (1993). "Adoption: Overview and Major Recommendations." *The Future of Children 3,* 4-16.

Schwartz, L. L. (1983). "Contested Adoption Cases: Grounds for Conflict between Psychology and the Law." *Professional Psychology: Research and Practice 14,* 444-56.

Shalev, C. (1989). *Birth Power: The Case for Surrogacy.* New Haven: Yale University Press.

Shorter, E. (1975). *The Making of the Modern Family.* New York: Basic.

Silverman, D. (1989). "The Impossible Dreams of Reformism and Romanticism." In J. F. Gubrium and D. Silverman (eds.), *The Politics of Field Research: Sociology beyond Enlightenment*, pp. 30–48. London: Sage.

Simanek, S. E. (1983). "Adoption Records Reform: Impact on Adoptees." *Marquette Law Review 67*, 110–46.

Simon, N. N., and Senturia, A. G. (1966). "Adoption and Psychiatric Illness." *American Journal of Psychiatry 122*, 858–68.

Simons, H. W. (1970). "Requirement, Problems, and Strategies: A Theory of Persuasion for Social Movements." *Quarterly Journal of Speech 54*, 1–11.

Skolnick, A. (1991). *Embattled Paradise: The American Family in an Age of Uncertainty.* New York: Basic.

Slagle, A. D. (n.d.). "The Eight Great Fallacies of Adoption." New York: The ALMA Society.

Smelser, N. J. (1992). "Culture: Coherent or Incoherent." In R. Munch and N. J. Smelser (eds.), *Theory of Culture*, pp. 3–21. Berkeley: University of California Press.

Smith, D. E. (1987). *The Everyday World as Problematic: A Feminist Sociology.* Boston: Northeastern University Press.

Smith, M. J. (1982). *Persuasion and Human Action: A Review and Critique of Social Influence Theories.* Belmont, Calif.: Wadsworth.

Smith, R. R., and Windes, R. R. (1976). "The Rhetoric of Mobilization: Implications for the Study of Movements," *Southern Speech Communication Journal 42*, 1–19.

Snook, L. (1973). "Thoughts on Myths and Their Meaning" (program notes). *Richard Wagner: Siegfried/Recorded Live at Beyreuth Festival, 1966.* Haarlem, the Netherlands: Phillips Records.

Snow, D. A., Rochford, E. B., Jr., Worden, S. K., and Benford, R. D. (1986). "Frame Alignment Processes, Micromobilization, and Movement Participation." *American Sociological Review 51*, 464–81.

Sobol, M. P., and Cardiff, J. (1983). "A Socio-psychological Investigation of Adult Adoptees' Search for Birth Parents." *Family Relations 32*, 477–83.

Solinger, R. (1992). *Wake Up Little Susie: Single Pregnancy and Race before Roe V. Wade.* New York: Routledge.

——— (1994). "Race and 'Value': Black and White Illegitimate Babies, 1945–1965." In E. N. Glenn, C. Chang, and L. R. Forcey (eds.), *Mothering: Ideology, Experience and Agency*, pp. 287–310. New York: Routledge.

Sonya Live (1992). "The Legal Effects of the Gregory Kingsley Trial on Adoption." Cable News Network. September 25, transcript 142.

—— (1994). "Whose Am I?" Cable News Network. March 14, transcript 504.

Sorich, C. J., and Siebert, R. (1982). "Toward Humanizing Adoption." *Child Welfare 61*, 207-16.

Sorosky, A., Baran, A., and Pannor, R. (1975). "Identity Conflicts in Adoptees." *American Journal of Orthopsychiatry 45*, 18-27.

Stack, C. B. (1975). *All Our Kin: Strategies for Survival in a Black Community.* New York: Harper and Row.

Stein, L. M., and Hoopes, J. L. (1985). *Identity Formation in the Adopted Adolescent.* New York: Child Welfare League of America.

Stewart, B. J. (1990). "Adoption, Personality Disorder and Parental Guilt: Implications of Genetic Research for Social Work." *Child and Adolescent Social Work 7*, 233-46.

Stolley, K. S. (1993). "Statistics on Adoption in the United States." *The Future of Children 3*, 483-92.

Stoneman, A. H. (1926). "Adoption of Illegitimate Children: The Peril in Ignorance." *Child Welfare League of America Bulletin 5*, 8.

Tartanella, P. J. (1982). "Sealed Adoption Records and the Constitutional Right of Privacy of the Natural Parent." *Rutgers Law Review 34*, 451-90.

Tate, T. (1990). "Trafficking in Children for Adoption." In C. Moorehead (ed.), *Betrayal: A Report on Violence toward Children in Today's World,* pp. 143-65. New York: Doubleday.

Taylor, E. (1989). "Are You My Mother?" *Time,* October 9, 90.

Teichman, J. (1982). *Illegitimacy: An Examination of Bastardy.* Ithaca: Cornell University Press.

Terrell, J., and Modell, J. (1994). "Anthropology and Adoption." *American Anthropologist 96*, 155-61.

Thornburn, D. (1987). "Television as an Aesthetic Medium." *Critical Studies in Mass Communication 4*, 161-73.

Toussieng, P. W. (1962). "Thoughts Regarding the Etiology of Psychological Difficulties in Adopted Children." *Child Welfare 41*, 59-65.

Trilling, L. (1972). *Sincerity and Authenticity.* Cambridge: Harvard University Press.

Triseliotis, J. (1973). *In Search of Origins: The Experiences of Adopted People.* London: Routledge.

—— (1984). "Obtaining Birth Certificates." In P. Bean (ed.), *Adoption: Essays in Social Policy, Law and Sociology,* pp. 38-53. London: Tavistock.

———— (1991). "Identity and Genealogy in Adopted People." In E. D. Hibbs (ed.), *Adoption: International Perspectives,* pp. 35–44. Madison, Conn.: International University Press.

———— (1993). "Inter-country Adoption: In Whose Best Interest?" In M. Humphrey and H. Humphrey (eds.), *Inter-country adoption: Practical Experiences,* pp. 119–37. London: Routledge.

Tuchman, G. (1974). "Assembling a Network Talk Show." In G. Tuchman (ed.), *The TV Establishment: Programming for Power and Profit,* pp. 119–35. Englewood Cliffs: Prentice-Hall.

Ussher, J. M. (1989). *The Psychology of the Female Body.* New York: Routledge.

Walker, N. A. (1991). "Introduction." *Women's Studies 22,* 1–4.

Wall Street Journal (1989). July 28.

Watson, K. (1992). "Keynote Address to the North American Council for Adoptable Children." *Adoptalk,* Fall, 2.

Weedon, C. (1987). *Feminist Practice and Poststructuralist Theory.* New York: Basil Blackwell.

Wegar, K. (1992). "The Sociological Significance of Ambivalence: An Example from Adoption Research." *Qualitative Sociology 15,* 87–103.

Weigert, A. J. (1991). *Mixed Emotions: Certain Steps toward Understanding Ambivalence.* Albany: State University of New York Press.

Weigert, A. J., and Franks, D. D. (1989). "Ambivalence: A Touchstone of the Modern Temper." In D. D. Franks and E. D. McCarthy (eds.), *The Sociology of Emotions: Original Essays and Research Papers,* pp. 205–27. Greenwich, Conn.: JAI Press.

West, C. (1990). "The New Cultural Politics of Difference." In R. Ferguson, M. Gever, T. T. Minha, and C. West (eds.), *Out There: Marginalization and Contemporary Cultures,* pp. 19–36. Cambridge: MIT Press.

Whitmore, H. S. (1959). "To My Adopted Daughter: I Wish I Hadn't Told You." *McCall's,* September, 66–67.

"Why Did My Mother Give Me Away?" (1965). *New York Times Magazine,* January 24.

Williams, L. S. (1990). "Motherhood, Ideology, and the Power of Technology: In Vitro Fertilization Use by Adoptive Mothers." *Women's Studies International Forum 13,* 543–52.

Work, H. H., and Anderson, H. (1971). "Studies in Adoption: Requests for Psychiatric Treatment." *American Journal of Psychiatry 127,* 948–50.

Wuthnow, R. (1987). *Meaning and Moral Order: Explorations in Cultural Analysis.* Berkeley: University of California Press.

Zeilinger, R. (1979). "The Need vs. the Right to Know." *Public Welfare 37*, 44–47.

Zelizer, V. A. (1985). *Pricing the Priceless Child: The Changing Social Value of Children*. New York: Basic.

Zola, I. K. (1987). " 'Any Distinguishing Features?' The Portrayal of Disability in the Crime-Mystery Genre." *Policy Studies Journal 15*, 485–513.

INDEX

AAC. *See* American Adoption Congress

Abortion debate, 11, 127–29

"Adopted child syndrome," 46, 56–58

Adoptees. *See* Adult adoptees; Interests of the child

Adoptees-in-Search, 17

Adoptees' Liberty Movement Association (ALMA), 2, 17, 84, 116

Adoption: as alternative to abortion, 127–29; as alternative to assisted reproduction, 129–30; ancient patterns of, 23–24; cultural inequalities and, 35–39; institutionalization of, 23–25; lack of sociological interest in, 5–8; between related parties, 21n; state legislation on, 3–4; statistics on, 21–22. *See also* Independent adoption; International adoption; Transracial adoption

Adoption agency practices: changes in, 43–44; disclosure and, 20–21, 30; guarantees of confidentiality and, 32, 40–41, 43; principle of confidentiality and, 32, 41, 61; professionalization of social work and, 47–52,

124; sealed records statutes and, 30; variation in, 4–5. *See also* American adoption system

Adoption research: on birth mothers, 52–55; genetic factors and, 61; impact of *Shared Fate* and, 58–61; multidimensional approach in, 60; need to search and, 61–67; psychopathological model and, 45–47, 55–58, 60; "scientism" and, 94, 95–96; sociopsychological model of, 47, 61–71. *See also* Expert opinion

Adoptive mother: normative assumptions about mothering and, 125, 133; psychopathological approach and, 55–58; social position of, 38–39, 91–92, 133; stigma of infertility and, 36–37, 58, 60, 91–92, 133

Adoptive parents: "adopted child syndrome" and, 46, 56–58; adoption system and, 50, 60, 134; child abuse and, 89–90; coping strategies of, 59–60; in dramatic structure of search narrative, 85–86; emotional problems among, 51–52, 56–57; ethic of reciprocity and, 80–81; father's infertility and, 91–92; need to search and, 63–64; represen-

know and, 2, 61–67, 66n, 90,
130–34; right to know and, 3,
17, 32, 33–34, 61–62, 134–38. *See
also* Confidentiality; Disclosure;
Identity development; Sealed
records policy
Birth mother: adoptee's post-
reunion relationship with,
65; adoption as alternative to
abortion and, 128–29; cultural
attitudes toward, 37–38, 52, 106;
feminist thinking and, 123–27;
in *Innocent Blood*, 104–5, 106;
relinquishment issues and, 38,
53–55; research on, 52–55
Birth parents: consequences of
sealed records policy for, 18–
19; genetic information and, 55;
mutual-consent registries and,
33; research on birth fathers and,
55; reunions and, 109, 117–18; as
search activists, 4
Bolen, Jean Shinoda, 100
Bosk, C. L., 78
Brodzinsky, David, 60
Burgess, Linda, 53
Burke, Kenneth, 10, 77n, 79n, 85
Burton, Tim, 98
Bush, George, 128

Canada, 63
Cashman, F., 21n
Cathcart, R., 77n
Chesler, Phyllis, 7, 90
Child. *See* Interests of the child
Child abuse, 89–90
Children's rights, 39–40
Child Welfare League of America,
4, 20–21, 25, 49, 54, 62, 70
Child welfare professionals. *See*

Adoption agency practices;
Social workers
Civil rights movement, 19–20
Class: adoption practice and, 35–
36, 55, 125; sealed records laws
and, 35–37, 38; searchers and, 63
Cognitive dissonance theory, 15n
Collective identity, 8–9, 73–74, 79,
96, 122
Concerned United Birthparents
(CUB), 4, 18n, 41
Condit, Celeste, 11
Confessional mode, 117–18
Confidentiality: agency guarantees
and, 32, 40–41, 43; decision of
birth mother and, 128–29; interests of parents and, 32–33; right
to search and, 61–62; vs. secrecy,
82–85; social workers' support
of, 28–29, 41, 61. *See also* Privacy,
right to; Sealed records policy
Constitutional issues: *See* Privacy,
right to; Property rights
Constructionist approach: life
stories and, 9, 79, 107–8; social
construction of kinship and,
23–24, 46–47, 67; social construction of mothering and,
123–27; statistics and, 22n. *See
also* Cultural factors; Identity
development; Social influences
"Conversion narrative," 87–88
Crane, Anne, 28
CUB. *See* Concerned United
Birthparents
Cullom, Donna, 76
Cultural factors: American model
of adoption and, 25–29, 118–
19; ideological uniformity and,
109–10; images of adoptees and,

hood and, 123–27; reproductive technologies and, 129–30

Fisher, Florence, 2, 18, 83, 131; *The Search for Anna Fisher,* 75, 84, 85, 87

Flexner, Abraham, 48

Foster, Austin, 29, 82

Foster care system, 35

Found stories, 76

Frame-critical perspective, xi, 10n, 34–35. *See also* Framing

Framing: controversies and, 10–13; role of media and, 107–8; search narratives and, 76–77, 108; strategies in disclosure debate and, 82–85

Freedman, Daniel, 102

Freidson, E., 48n

Freud, Anna, 26–27

Functionalist approach, 47n

Gamete donation, and anonymity, 129, 130

Gender: as issue in adoption, 37–39, 54–55, 124–25; number of female searchers and, 65; responses to infertility and, 133–34; sociological inquiry and, 74n; women as mothers and, 58. *See also* Feminist scholarship; Motherhood

Genealogical information, 18–20, 33–34, 68, 96, 111, 137

Genetic factors: in adoption, 43–44, 50, 55, 59; adoption research and, 61; importance in human behavior, 102

Geraldo (television show), 111–18

Gerbner, George, 110

Gesell, Arnold, 48

Gilligan, Carol, 65

Glenn, Norval, 120

Goffman, Erving, 132

Goldstein, Joseph, 26–27

Good cause standard, 30–31, 32, 33–34, 68

"Good mothering," 124–25

Gordon, Linda, 37

Gray, Laura, 116, 117

Great Britain: assisted reproduction policy in, 130; legislation in, 24, 26, 70–71, 118; searchers in, 63, 70–71. See also *Innocent Blood*

Griffin, C. J. G., 87n

Gusfield, Joseph, 16, 93

Haimes, Erica, 36–37, 71, 130

Heredity. *See* Genetic factors

Hilgartner, S., 78

Holocaust metaphor, 88–89

Hoopes, Janet L., 131

Humphrey, Heather, 103

Humphrey, Michael, 103

Identity development: creation of identity and, 83, 118–19; differences among adoptees and, 13–14, 64; ethic of self-discovery and, 81–82; ethnic identity and, 68n, 73; genetic factors and, 44, 68; good cause standard and, 33–34; impact of stigmatization on, 132–34; importance of genealogical knowledge and, 18, 33–34, 68; interactionist approach to, 130–34, 136, 138; search-movement rhetoric and, 78–79, 81–82, 94–95; search stories in popular culture and,

Identity development (*continued*)
97–98, 101–2; social construction
of kinship and, 23–24, 34–35

Ideology, 15, 24, 109–10, 123–24.
See also American family ideology; Cultural factors; Feminist
scholarship

Illegitimacy, 7, 101, 116; attitudes
toward, 26, 36–38, 124; women's
experience and, 126

Incest taboo, 106–7

Independent adoption, 21–22, 50,
69–70

Individualism: vs. individuality, 80;
sealed records debate and, 82–83,
118–19, 136

Individualization of adoption
issues, 99, 108, 117–18, 136

Inequalities in adoption system, 6,
35–39, 52–53, 54–55

Infertility: fathers and, 91–92;
psychodynamic approach and,
56, 58–59; as stigma, 36–37, 58,
60, 91–92, 133–34

Informal adoption, 24, 36

Inheritance rights, 25

Innocent Blood (James), 98, 102–7

Interactionist approach: need
to know and, 130–34; right to
know and, 134–38

Interests of the child: adoption
legislation and, 4, 24, 25–29;
ethic of reciprocity and, 80–81;
as legal notion, 26–27; media
focus and, 109; sealed records
practices and, 28–29

International adoption, 36, 109

International Soundex Reunion
Registry, 63

James, P. D., 98, 102–7
Johnson, T., 52n
Jones, Mary Ann, 61

Kansas Supreme Court, 27
King, Martin Luther, 11
Kinship: adoption as absence of,
89–90; biocentric bias and, 6–7,
13, 28, 34–35, 40, 41, 73, 89–92;
incest taboo and, 106–7; natural
vs. social elements of, 13–16, 41–
42, 99, 110, 126; search stories in
popular culture and, 97–98, 99,
103, 111–13; social construction
of, 23–24, 46–47, 60, 67. *See
also* American family ideology;
Parenthood

Kirk, H. David, 5, 7, 43–44, 47–48,
58–61, 119

Kirschner, David, 46, 57–58

Legislation on adoption: history
of, 3–4, 24–25; incest taboo
and, 106–7; interests of the
child and, 24, 25–29; states with
open records laws, 3; statutes vs.
agency practice and, 30–31. *See
also* Sealed records policy

Life stories. *See* Search narratives

Lifton, Betty Jean: on desire to
search, 123; Holocaust metaphor
and, 89; on motherhood, 91;
on need for birth knowledge, 2,
66n, 90; on own search, 84, 87;
on secrecy argument, 86; as talk
show guest, 115–16; *Twice Born*,
75, 82

Lindee, Susan, 41, 86

Literary works, adoption themes

Nelkin, Dorothy, 41, 86
Neo-Weberian approach, 47n, 48n
New Yorker, 118–19
New York state, 30–31
New York State Registry, 18
Nobody's Child (Balter), 132
Nonsearchers: conversion narrative and, 88; experiences of, 63, 66, 114–15, 123; mental health problems and, 66n, 72, 123
North American Council on Adoptable Children, 61

Open adoption, 3, 20, 32–33
Opposition to reform: ethic of reciprocity and, 80–81; rhetorical strategies of, 92–96. *See also* Confidentiality; Expert opinion; Social workers
Oprah Winfrey Show, 111, 120
Orphan Voyage, 19

Pannor, Reuben, 62, 64
Parens patriae, principle of, 27, 83–84
Parenthood: parent-child bonding and, 110, 111–12, 113; psychological parenting concept and, 26–27; social vs. biological, 89–92. *See also* Adoptive mother; Adoptive parents; American family ideology; Birth mother; Birth parents; Fathers; Kinship; Motherhood
Paton, Jean, 18–19, 32, 72, 75
Periodicals, adoption stories in, 75–76, 102, 109
Pierce, William, 113–14
Political symbolism, 82–85, 113
Popular culture, adoption in, 97–

120; See also *Innocent Blood;* Media; *Siegfried;* Talk shows
Privacy, right to: birth parents and, 26, 32, 33; sealed records policy as violation of, 17, 31; search as violation of, 112–13
Professionalization of social work: guarantees of confidentiality and, 28, 40–41, 43; psychomedical model and, 40–41, 47–52; theories of professions and, 47nn. *See also* Expert opinion; Social workers
Property rights, 26, 27–28, 51n, 83–84
Psychodynamic model, 50–51, 52–53, 55–56
Psychological parenting concept, 26–27
Psychopathological model, 45–47, 55–58, 67–69, 135. *See also* Mental health problems

Racial inequalities, 36, 52–53, 54–55. *See also* Transracial adoption
Rapping, Elayne, 6
Reagan, Ronald, 127
Reciprocity, ethic of, 80–81
Reitz, Miriam, 64
Relinquishment issues, 38, 53–55
Reunions: individualization of reactions to, 117–18; life stories and, 96, 109; sealed records policy and, 62–63; variation among outcomes, 65. *See also* Talk shows
Rhetoric: constructionist approach and, 9–10; difference as context and, 2–3; interactionist approach and, 137–38; managerial vs.

confrontational, 77n; moral vocabularies of motive and, 78–82; opposition to reform and, 92–96. *See also* Framing; Search narratives

Riben, Marsha, 88, 89–90

Rights. *See* Abortion debate; Birth information; Natural rights doctrine; Privacy, right to; Property rights

Ring of the Nibelungen (Wagner), 100

Rolfe, Randy, 114

Roman law, 23, 24, 25

Rosenwald, George C., 78

Rothman, Barbara Katz, 124, 126, 137

Sachdev, Paul, 65

Sally Jessy Raphael (television show), 111, 112–13

Schaefer, Carol, 75

Schechter, Marshall, 45, 51, 56

Schneider, David, 41

"Scientism," 94–96. *See also* Expert opinion; Psychopathological model

Sealed records policy, 1–5; bases for opposition to, 17–18; biocentric bias and, 40; child's interests as motivation for, 25–29, 40; class discrimination and, 35–37, 40; confidentiality vs. secrecy and, 84–85; constitutional issues and, 31–32; definitions of motherhood and, 123–27; ethos of individualism and, 82–83; as focus of search debate, 30; good cause standard and, 26, 30–31, 32, 33–34; interactionist

approach and, 134–38; media attention and, 113–14; natural vs. social elements of kinship and, 13–16; need to search and, 62–63; origins of debate and, 17–42; policy alternatives and, 134–38; professional status of social workers and, 28, 40–41, 69–70; reunion outcomes and, 62–63; statutes vs. adoption agency practice and, 4–5, 30–31; Uniform Adoption Act and, 3, 21, 63. *See also* Mutual-consent registries; Opposition to reform; Search movement

Search debate. *See* Birth information; Disclosure; Opposition to reform; Sealed records policy; Search movement

Searching: adoption agency involvement in, 62–63, 70–71; characteristics of searchers, 63–64; cultural representations of, 98–120; experiences of nonsearchers and, 63, 66, 114–15, 123; motives behind, 64–65, 78–82, 117–18; as natural, 61–62, 66; number of searchers, 22, 63; reunion outcomes and, 62–63, 65

Search movement: adoption agencies and, 30, 69–70; adoptive family relationships and, 130–31; civil rights movement and, 19–20; collective identity and, 8–9, 73–74, 122; cultural images of adoptees and, 72–74, 98, 121–23; development of, 17–22; difference and, 2–3, 121–23; expert opinion and, 12–13, 67–71, 94–96, 114–15; first search group

Search movement (*continued*)
and, 19; focus on laws vs. practice and, 30; media attention and, 107–9, 111; moral vocabularies of motive and, 78–82; need to search and, 61–62, 66; number of searchers and, 22, 63; politics of search narratives and, 74–78; right to know and, 134–35; as social movement, 8–10, 73; stereotypes about adoption and, 124. *See also* Mutual-consent registries; Sealed records policy

Search narratives: confessional mode and, 116–18; "conversion narrative" and, 87–88; dramatic structure of, 85–89; "found stories" and, 76; new social movements and, 8–9; politics of, 72–73, 74–78; reunion narrative and, 109; search movement and, 72–73

Secrecy: adoption theme in literature and, 101; vs. confidentiality, 82–85; media attention and, 108

Self-discovery, ethic of, 81–82, 119

Shalev, Carmel, 38

Shared Fate (Kirk), 43–44, 47–48, 58–61

Siegfried (Wagner), 98, 99–101

Single mothers. *See* Illegitimacy

Single-parent adoption, 108, 125

Smith, Dorothy, 74n

Social control perspective, 37–38, 39–42, 52–53, 124

Social influences: attitudes toward adoptive families and, 59–60; confessional mode in talk shows and, 117–18; psychopathological model and, 52, 57–58;

"scientism" and, 94, 95–96; social construction of kinship and, 23–24, 46–47, 60, 67. *See also* Constructionist approach; Cultural factors; Stigmatization

Social movements, new, 8, 73, 74–78

Social problem, concept of, 7, 68n

Social workers: attitudes toward adoptive families and, 59–60; debate over disclosure among, 20–21; gender issues and, 124–25; involvement in search process, 62–63, 70–71; need to search and, 61–62; professional status and, 28, 40–41, 43, 47–52, 70; search activists and, 4–5, 69–70; support for confidentiality among, 28–29, 32–33, 43, 61. *See also* Adoption agency practices

Sociologists, 5–8, 74n. *See also* Constructionist approach; Interactionist approach; *Shared Fate*; Social influences

Sociopsychological model, 47, 61–71

Solinger, Rickie, 53

Solnit, Albert, 26–27

Sonya Live (television show), 113–14, 115–16, 117

Sorosky, Arthur, 62, 64

Special-needs children, 108

Statistics: on adoption, 21–22; in search debate, 93–94

Stein, Leslie M., 131

Steinberg, Lisa, 88, 89

Stereotypes, 58, 106, 122, 124–25

Stigmatization: adoption research and, 47, 52, 58, 60, 102, 132–33; adoptive parents' reactions to